Bible
MEDITATIONS
for all your needs

Bible
MEDITATIONS
for all your needs

Lloyd Hildebrand

BRIDGE
LOGOS

Alachua, Florida 32615

Bridge-Logos

Alachua, FL 32615 USA

Bible Meditations For All Your Needs

by Lloyd Hildebrand

Printed in the United States of America.

Library of Congress Catalog Card Number: 2015932691

International Standard Book Number: 978-1-61036-141-5

Unless otherwise noted, all Scripture quotations are from the King James Version of the Holy Bible.

Cover Design: Paul Hildebrand

03-03-15

DEDICATION

TO all of my students and readers. You are a blessing to me!

CONTENTS

INTRODUCTION

❧

"LET THE WORDS OF MY MOUTH, and the meditation of my heart, be acceptable in thy sight, O Lord, my strength and my redeemer" (Psalm 19:14).

I love God's Word, and I marvel over its power to change people's lives. Learning to meditate upon the Bible has certainly brought lasting and positive changes to my life, and I know it will do the same for you.

The Bible is far more than just a compilation of words. It contains the answer to every human need. Great spiritual discernment is given to all who learn to meditate upon its truths. The Bible says, "But the natural man receiveth not the things of the Spirit of God: for they are foolishness unto him: neither can he know them, because they are spiritually discerned" (1 Corinthians 2:14).

Pray for spiritual discernment as you engage in Bible meditation. I can assure you that it will come to you and the result will be wisdom, peace, and victory in your life.

Meditating on the life-changing words of God is a wellspring of spiritual power for your life. It will change your heart and your mind. There are many possible focal points of Bible meditation, and some of these are:

- The blessings of God in your life. Remember, He daily loads you with benefits. (See Psalm 68:19.)
- The steadfast love of God.
- The Word of God and the specific words of God.
- God's help in your life.
- The marvelous works of the Lord.
- God's majestic splendor and miracle-working power.
- God's works.
- The promises of God to you.
- God's holy name.
- Who you are in and through Jesus Christ.

"For the word of God is quick and powerful, and sharper than any twoedged sword, piercing even to the dividing asunder of soul and spirit, and of the joints and marrow, and is a discerner of the thoughts and intents of the heart" (Hebrews 4:12).

The above list provides us with only some of the focal points of meditation in our lives. As we read the Psalms, for example, we are reminded by the word *Selah* to pause and calmly reflect on what God is saying to us. (This is true Bible meditation.)

Selah! This word tells us to meditate upon what we've just read. Remember *Selah* as you read God's Word. The Bible says, "Be still, and know that I am God" (Psalm 46:10). Isaiah wrote, "In quietness and in confidence shall be your strength" (Isaiah 30:15).

It's very important to be still and quiet before God as you meditate upon His truths and promises.

What are some of the results of pausing and reflecting on the Scriptures as the word Selah directs us to do?

- You will be reminded of all God has done, is doing, and will do in your life.
- He will bring to your remembrance the truths He has imparted to you.
- Your love for God and His Word will grow, and your faith will increase.
- You will receive spiritual understanding and greater wisdom.
- It will lead you to pray according to His Word and will. (See 1 John 5:14-15.)
- It will lead you to share His truths with others.

- It will produce joy in your heart.
- It will bring comfort to you.
- It will give you a peace that surpasses all understanding. (See Philippians 4:7.)

Each of the meditations within this book is personal and specific. The Word of God forms the core of each meditation. All the Scriptures involved with each meditation are listed as references for your further study.

As you practice meditation on God's Word, be sure to take time to ponder each truth that is revealed. Make sure you are in a quiet place and are listening for God's voice. He will speak to you through His Word and through that "still, small voice." (See 1 Kings 19:12.)

Don't forget that throughout this book God will be speaking directly to you. Be sure to take time to listen and to apply His truths to your life. Jesus said, "My sheep hear my voice, and I know them, and they follow me" (John 10:27).

As you discover the power of Bible meditation for your own life, you will become ". . . like a tree planted by the rivers of water, that bringeth forth his fruit in his season" (Psalm 1:3).

I've experienced the power of God's Word over and over again in every area of my life. I cherish its words and I believe its promises. I want the same for you, and I know this is God's will for you.

John wrote, "These things have I written unto you that believe on the name of the Son of God; that ye may know that ye have eternal life, and that ye may believe on the name of the Son of God. And this is the confidence that we have in him, that, if we ask any thing according to his will, he heareth us: And if we know that he hear us, whatsoever we ask, we know that we have the petitions that we desired of him" (1 John 5:13-15).

As you read God's Word, meditate upon its truths. As you meditate upon God's Word, pray it back to Him. As you pray His promises, take hold of them. In this way your faith will soar and your heart will be free.

Andrew Murray advised, ". . . holding the Word of God in your heart until it has affected every phase of your life." This is the desired result of meditation—to get the Word of God into your heart so that it affects everything you do--what you say, what you think, what you feel, what you pray, and what you desire.

You are about to be richly blessed as you use the meditations in this book. May they lead you closer to the Lord each day of your life, and may you experience the power of Bible meditation throughout your life and in every situation of your life.

Part I

———— ∞∞∞ ————

You Can Trust God's Word

Let thy mercies come also unto me, O Lord,
even thy salvation, according to thy word.
So shall I have wherewith to answer him that
reproacheth me: for I trust in thy word.
And take not the word of truth utterly out of
my mouth; for I have hoped in thy judgments.
(Psalm 119:41–43)

Meditating on God's Word is one of life's most enjoyable and energizing experiences. Joshua wrote, "This Book of the Law [the Bible] shall not depart from your mouth, but you shall meditate in it day and night, that you may observe to do according to all that is written in it. For then you will make your way prosperous, and then you will have good success" (Joshua 1:8, NKJV).

This verse shows us what happens when we meditate upon the Scriptures and what we can expect to happen as we learn their teachings, and apply them to our lives. When we do so, the Bible promises that we will prosper and be successful. Bible meditation is such an important activity, because it results in so many blessings both in this life and the life that is to come.

What is Bible meditation? It is the process that enables us to focus our thoughts on God's Word, to reflect on its truths, and to contemplate its meaning for our lives. The word *meditation* is derived from the Hebrew word *hagah* which has several interpretations: to mutter, to bow down, to muse, to murmur, to converse with oneself (aloud), to speak, to babble, to communicate, to groan, and to roar.

The concept of meditation, therefore, may involve all these activities, and each one has to do with the gift of speech and communication. One might wonder how roaring, for example, could possibly be involved with meditation, which seems to connote a peaceful manner and attitude. However, in the case of spiritual warfare, it is easy to see how roaring might be involved as we take a stand against the enemy.

The idea of muttering God's Word suggests a

repetitious process of proclaiming the truths and promises of the Bible in the face of any and all circumstances. It involves uttering God's words aloud, sometimes softly, sometimes loudly, but always with the confidence and authority that come from God's Word.

J.I. Packer has written, "Meditation is the activity of calling to mind, thinking over, dwelling on, and applying to oneself the various things one knows about the works and ways and purpose and promises of God. . . .It is an activity of holy thought, consciously performed in the presence of God, under the eye of God, by the help of God, as a means of communion with God."

SPEAKING FORTH GOD'S WORD

Paul wrote, "The word is near you, in your mouth and in your heart" (Romans 10:8, NKJV). Why is speaking God's Word such an important part of meditation? It's because we remember ten percent of what we read, twenty percent of what we hear, thirty percent of what we see, and seventy percent of what we speak. Therefore, as we meditate upon the truths and precepts of Scripture, it is often important to speak God's Word aloud.

Doing so helps us to memorize the Word of God. As we speak it forth from our hearts as a result of

9

this process, God hears us and responds to His Word as it is being proclaimed. His angels respond as well. Isaiah writes, "So shall My word be that goes forth from My mouth; it shall not return to Me void, but it shall accomplish what I please. And it shall prosper in the thing for which I sent it" (Isaiah 55:11, NKJV).

Speaking God's Word, as we meditate upon its principles, reinforces its truth to our hearts and gives us courage and strength. God loves to hear His words spoken back to Him, because He knows how important doing so is to us.

In many ways, Bible meditation is like a cow chewing its cud, swallowing it, regurgitating it, and swallowing it again. Bible meditation enables us to reflect on the truths of God's Word over and over again and to let it become a vital part of our lives. These truths are there for us to reflect upon as often as necessary, because they are lodged deep within us.

Meditation is chewing on the Word, ruminating on its teachings, pondering its truth, analyzing its intentions, personalizing its promises, and acting upon its commandments.

C.H. Spurgeon wrote, "Have you a spiritual taste, dear hearer? It is one thing to hear the Word. It is another thing to taste it. Hearing the Word is often blessed, but tasting it is a more inward and spiritual thing—it is the enjoyment of the Truth in the innermost parts of our being! Oh, that we were all as fond of the Word as were the old mystics who chewed the cud of meditation till they were fattened upon the Word of God and their souls grew strong in the divine love! I am sure of this—the more you know of God's Word, the more you will love it."

Here are some scriptural passages that deal with Bible meditation:

"When I remember thee upon my bed, and meditate on thee in the night watches" (Psalm 63:6). Yes, we should meditate upon the Lord himself, beholding Him with the eyes of our spirits and gazing upon His beauty, His glory, and His radiance both day and night.

"Bless the Lord, O my soul: and all that is within me, bless his holy name. Bless the Lord, O my soul, and forget not all his benefits" (Psalm 103:1-2). Let us meditate upon His multiple blessings in our life. Counting your blessings is so much better than seeing problems only, and doing so enables us to rise above the circumstances in which we find ourselves.

"O how love I thy law! It is my meditation all the day" (Psalm 119:97). Meditating upon the Word of God brings great joy and peace to us. It is something we can do and should do all day long. The Bible says, "Thou wilt shew me the path of life: in thy presence is fullness of joy; at thy right hand there are pleasures for evermore" (Psalm 16:11). Fullness of joy and pleasures forevermore will be yours as you learn to practice God's presence by meditating upon His Word.

"We have thought of thy lovingkindness, O God, in the midst of thy temple" (Psalm 48:9). As we think of and contemplate the love of God, we are changed and blessed. We are filled with God's peace and joy. There is nothing more wonderful to contemplate than the love God has for us. His love casts all fear away from us.

There are many other passages in the Bible that deal with meditation, and, though the focal points of our meditation may change, we greatly benefit from this process of mental renewal and physical reenergizing. So engage in Bible meditation every day. Meditate upon Him, your blessings, His living Word, His never-ending love, His miracles and wonderful works in your life, His splendor, His principles, His help in your life, His majesty, His glory, His holy name, His promises, and all He is to you.

"Meditation is a way of slowing down so as to descend into the depths of yourself in the present moment, where God lies waiting to grant you a deep experience of your eternal oneness with God" (James Finley).

BIBLE MEDITATION PRODUCES IMPORTANT CHANGES IN YOUR LIFE

Meditation will lead you to love God's Word, and loving God's Word will lead you into spiritual meditation. It will result in total transformation in your life.

As you meditate on God's Word, these are some of the things that will change in your life:

- Your memory will improve, as you recall all He has done for you.
- Your mind will be renewed as you realize what a treasure God's Word is to you and you reflect upon its wisdom and apply it to your life.
- You will experience the love of God deep within your spirit in ways you've never experienced before.
- Your spiritual understanding of the things of God will greatly improve.

- You will be comforted by the God of all comfort.
- You will learn to be an effective witness, one who shares God's Word with others.
- Praise and worship will arise from deep within your heart.
- Your joy will be full.
- You will discern the voice of the Lord.
- Your heart will be in tune with God's will and His ways.
- You will engage in prayer and cultivate intimacy with the Father.
- You will experience God's peace that surpasses all understanding.
- You will hide God's Word in your heart so as to not sin against Him.
- You will be enabled to rightly divide God's Word.
- You will be ready to give an answer to anyone who asks you about spiritual things.
- You will be instructed in righteousness, that you will be thoroughly furnished unto all good works.
- You will grow in the grace and knowledge of the Lord Jesus Christ.

- Your heart will stay in good spiritual health.
- Your soul will be fed.
- Your fellowship with Jesus and others will grow.

As you delve more deeply into Bible meditation, you will see other changes taking place as well. You will be thrilled to see God at work in your life.

"The heart is heated by meditation and cold truth is melted into passionate action" (Donald S. Whitney).

WHAT IS GOD'S WORD TO YOU?

Do you take delight in God's Word? Do you love the Word as the Psalmist did? In Psalm 119 we read these words: "I will meditate in thy precepts, and have respect unto thy ways. I will delight myself in thy statutes: I will not forget thy word" (Psalm 119:15-16). As you meditate upon His Word, your sense of delight will grow, and you will receive answers to your prayers.

As C.H. Spurgeon pointed out, there is a vast difference between reading God's Word and meditating upon it. He said, "I quarry out the truth when I read, but I smelt the ore and get the pure gold out of it when I meditate!" Meditation enables you to find veins of truth from which you will extract pure nuggets of gold.

Spurgeon also said, "For lack of meditation the truth of God runs by us and we miss and lose it. Our treacherous memory is like a sieve—and what we hear and what we read runs through it and leaves but little behind—and that little is often unprofitable to us by reason of our lack of diligence to get thoroughly at it. I often find it very profitable to get a text as a sweet morsel under my tongue in the morning and to keep the flavor of it, if I can, in my mouth all day."

Start your day with meditation upon God's Word, let that meditation continue throughout the day, and conclude the day in the same way. By so doing you will enjoy the flavor of the Word and let its spiritual nutrition sink into your soul and spirit.

Jesus said, "Come unto me, all ye that labour and are heavy laden, and I will give you rest. Take my yoke upon you, and learn of me; for I am meek and lowly in heart: and ye shall find rest unto your souls" (Matthew 11:28-29).

You will find Jesus in your meditation on the Scriptures, and He will give you rest. This is one aspect of Bible meditation that cannot be denied. The invitation is a simple one: "Come, and I will give you rest." However, the process is not easy, for it requires discipline, silence, and serious contemplation.

J.I. Packer wrote, "Meditation is not giving free rein to your imaginations, nor is it reading your Bible for beautiful thoughts. Meditation is a discipline."

Therefore, you need to discipline yourself to meditate upon God's Word, for His Word is. . .

- . . . a lamp unto your feet (Psalm 119:105)
- . . . a light unto your path (Psalm 119:105)
- . . . sharper than a two-edged sword (Hebrews 4:12)
- . . . like a hammer (Jeremiah 23:29)
- . . . the sword of the Spirit (Ephesians 6:17)
- . . . the Word of truth (John 17:17)
- . . . pure (Proverbs 30:5)
- . . . alive (1 Peter 1:23)
- . . . powerful (Hebrews 4:12)
- . . . like a fire (Jeremiah 23:29)
- . . . eternal (Isaiah 40:8)
- . . . good (Jeremiah 29:10)
- . . . faithful (Titus 1:9)
- . . . tried (Psalm 18:30)
- . . . settled in Heaven (Psalm 119:89)
- . . . enduring (1 Peter 1:25)

God's Word brings . . .

> . . . healing (Psalm 107:20)
>
> . . . instruction (2 Timothy 3:16)
>
> . . . quickening (Psalm 119:25)
>
> . . . hope (Psalm 119:114)
>
> . . . deliverance (Psalm 119:170)
>
> . . . faith (Romans 10:8)
>
> . . . cleansing (Ephesians 5:26)
>
> . . . sanctification (1 Timothy 4:5)

Apply God's Word to Your Life by. . .

> . . . reading it (1 Timothy 4:13)
>
> . . . meditating upon it (Psalm 119:47–48)
>
> . . . memorizing it (Psalm 119:11)
>
> . . . believing it (Romans 10:17)
>
> . . . obeying it (Deuteronomy 28:1)
>
> . . . rightly dividing it (2 Timothy 2:15)
>
> . . . speaking it forth (Romans 10:8)
>
> . . . studying it (2 Timothy 2:15)
>
> . . . praying it (1 John 5:14–15)

The Word of God is a treasure chest of truth, a flowing fountain of living water from which you may drink daily, a strong foundation on which you can build your life, a love letter from God to you, a fruitful tree of righteousness, a ladder that leads you to God's throne, a doorway that takes you into the very heart of God, an ocean of love, beauty, and wisdom, a deep well of salvation, and an unfailing source of comfort, hope, faith, victory, and prosperity for you.

"The Holy Scriptures are our letters from home" (Augustine of Hippo). In these letters you find promises from your Father who adopted you, and these are promises that you can surely count on. One of the most important effects of Bible meditation is getting to know its Author.

THE EFFECTS OF BIBLE MEDITATION

Charles Spurgeon wrote, "There are times when solitude is better than society, and silence is wiser than speech. We should be better Christians if we were more alone, waiting upon God, and gathering through meditation on His Word spiritual strength for labor in His service. We ought to muse upon the things of God, because we thus get the real nutriment out of them. . . . Why is it that some Christians, although they hear many sermons, make but slow advances in the divine life? Because they neglect their [prayer] closets, and do not thoughtfully meditate on God's Word. They love the wheat, but they do not grind it; they would have the corn, but they will not go forth into the fields to gather it; the fruit hangs upon

19

the tree, but they will not pluck it; the water flows at their feet, but they will not stoop to drink it. From such folly deliver us, O Lord."

The more you get into God's Word the more it gets into you. This will change your life in radical ways. You will become stronger, as did the young men described by the Apostle John: "I have written unto you, young men, because ye are strong, and the word of God abideth in you, and ye have overcome the wicked one" (1 John 2:14).

Through Bible meditation you are able to hear the Word and hearken unto it. Mixing your hearing of the Word with faith is a recipe that will bring tremendous blessing to your life. It will enable you to defeat the enemy whenever he comes with temptations.

Meditating upon God's Word is a powerful and effective way to incorporate its truths into your life. Paul wrote, "All scripture is given by inspiration of God, and is profitable for doctrine, for reproof, for correction, for instruction in righteousness: That the man of God may be perfect, thoroughly furnished unto all good works" (2 Timothy 3:16–17).

Meditating upon the Scriptures will help you to:

- Gain spiritual understanding
- Grow in wisdom

- Memorize God's Word
- Personalize God's Word
- Grow in grace
- Grow in faith
- Trust God
- Obey God's Word
- Go forth in victory
- Pray with confidence

As you meditate upon God's Word and follow its precepts, ask yourself the following questions regarding each passage:

- Are there any promises for me to claim?
- Do I need to change my attitude in any way?
- Are there any commands for me to obey?
- What does this passage teach me about Jesus Christ?
- Are there any errors for me to avoid?
- What does this passage teach me about my heavenly Father?
- How does this passage apply to my own life?
- Are there any sins that I must confess?

- What does this passage teach me about myself?
- What does this passage teach me about the world?
- How should my behavior change?
- Is there a truth that I should apply to my life?
- What does God say I should do?

V.C. Grounds wrote, "The Bible is more than just a record of long-ago events and ancient wisdom. It is the book that bears God's signature. It is His message of truth and grace to us. Let's not neglect it. Let's read it, believe it, and obey it." Let's also take the time to meditate upon each truth as if we were savoring a fine feast.

God is so good. He has provided you with so many tremendous resources that will help you to stay on track, keep you from falling, and help you maintain the victory in every area of your life.

Meditate upon God's Word. Savor it as you would a delicious morsel. Derive sustenance and strength from every bite you take from the Bible. It is then that God's Word will soak into your heart and mind and go to the innermost core of your being.

WALKING IN GOD'S WORD

Meditating upon God's Word will lead you to walk in His Word. It is a springboard for action. As a result, you will learn to walk . . .

> . . . before the Lord in the light of the living (Psalm 56:13)

> . . . uprightly (Proverbs 10:9)

> . . . surely (Proverbs 28:18)

> . . . in the light of the Lord (Isaiah 2:5)

> . . . in God's ways (Isaiah 30:21)

> . . . humbly with God (Micah 6:8)

> . . . in the steps of faith (Romans 4:12)

> . . . in newness of life (Romans 6:4)

> . . . after the Spirit (Romans 8:1)

> . . . by faith (2 Corinthians 5:7)

> . . . worthy of the vocation to which you have been called (Ephesians 4:1)

> . . . circumspectly (Ephesians 5:15)

> . . . worthy of the Lord (Colossians 1:10)

> . . . in the light (1 John 1:7)

When you walk in God's Word, His promises will become your stepping stones, and you will be able to walk securely, knowing that He will never let His Word return unto Him void. (See Isaiah 55:11.) It will enable you to hold ". . . forth the word

23

of life" (Philippians 2:16) and bring the Word of truth to people everywhere. (See James 1:18.)

Hide God's Word in your heart so that you will . . .

. . . not sin against Him (Psalm 119:11)

. . . pray His Word without
ceasing (1 Thessalonians 5:17)

. . . rejoice evermore (1 Thessalonians 5:16)

. . . be ready to give an answer to anyone
who asks you (1 Peter 3:15)

. . . resist the devil (James 4:7)

. . . grow in the grace and knowledge of the
Lord Jesus Christ (2 Peter 3:18)

. . . be taught the things of
God (2 Timothy 3:16)

. . . receive correction when
needed (2 Timothy 3:16)

. . . be instructed in
righteousness (2 Timothy 3:16)

. . . be approved unto God (2 Timothy 2:15)

. . . a workman who is never
ashamed (2 Timothy 2:15)

. . . rightly divide His Word (2 Timothy 2:15)

God's Word provides all these blessings for you, and much, much more. God's Word is . . .

. . . your offensive weapon—the sword of the

      Spirit. (See Ephesians 6:17.)

. . . more powerful than any two-edged
    sword. (See Hebrews 4:12.)

. . . a living Word. (See Hebrews 4:12.)

. . . like a fire. (See Jeremiah 23:29.)

. . . like a hammer. (See Jeremiah 23:29.)

. . . near you—in your mouth and upon your
    tongue. (See Romans 10:8.)

. . . eternal. (See Matthew 24:35.)

George Mueller, a man of uncommon faith and
exemplary Christian service, wrote about the
power of Bible meditation in his journal. This is
his entry for May 9, 1841: "It has pleased the Lord
to teach me a truth, the benefit of which I have
not lost for more than fourteen years. The point
is this: I saw more clearly than ever that the first
great and primary business to which I ought to
attend every day was to have my soul happy in
the Lord. . . not how much I might serve the Lord.
. . but how I might get my soul into a happy state,
and how my inner man might be nourished.

"For I might seek to set the truth before the
unconverted, I might seek to benefit believers. .
. and yet, not being happy in the Lord, and not
being nourished and strengthened in my inner
man day by day, all this might not be attended

to in a right spirit. Before this time my practice had been. . . to give myself to prayer after having dressed myself in the morning.

"Now, I saw that the most important thing I had to do was to give myself to the reading of the Word of God, *and to meditate upon it*, that thus my heart might be comforted, encouraged, warned, reproved, instructed; and that thus, by means of the Word of God, *whilst meditating upon it*, my heart might be brought into experimental communion with the Lord" (italics mine).

All these truths about God's Word show us why it is important to meditate upon His Word and to believe His promises. So much more could be said about the Scriptures, but let us conclude this chapter with these words from the Scriptures:

Let the word of Christ dwell in you richly in all wisdom; teaching and admonishing one another in psalms and hymns and spiritual songs, singing with grace in your hearts to the Lord. And whatsoever ye do in word or deed, do all in the name of the Lord Jesus, giving thanks to God and the Father by him.
(Colossians 3:16–17)

PART II

⸺ ❧ ⸺

THE POWER OF BIBLE MEDITATION

Those things, which ye have both learned, and received, and heard, and seen in me, do: and the God of peace shall be with you.

(Philippians 4:9)

THERE IS GREAT SPIRITUAL POWER to be derived from meditating on the Word of God. Through the process of meditation God changes us from the inside out. Our minds are renewed and our lives are transformed.

The Bible tells us to meditate upon:

- The Word of God. (See Joshua 1:8.)
- God's unfailing love. (See Psalm 48:9.)
- God's works and His mighty deeds. (See Psalm 77:12.)

- God's precepts and His ways. (See Psalm 119:15.)

- God's decrees. (See Psalm 119:23.)

- God's statutes. (See Psalm 119:23.)

- God's promises. (See Psalm 119:148.)

- God's wonderful works. (See Psalm 145:5.)

- Whatever is noble, right, pure, lovely and admirable. (See Philippians 4:8.)

Meditating on all these things (and other godly things, as well) will change our hearts and minds by providing us with God's wisdom and truth to apply to daily situations. It helps us to grow spiritually and to go deeper with God.

Isaiah wrote, "Thou wilt keep him in perfect peace, whose mind is stayed on thee: because he trusteth in thee" (Isaiah 26:3). As you focus on the Lord, you will experience His supernatural peace, His abiding joy, and His immeasurable love for you.

To meditate upon the Scriptures is to meditate upon the Lord.

What should we do in times of personal crisis? The Psalmist answers this question directly: "I hoped in thy word. Mine eyes prevent the night watches, that I might meditate in thy word. Hear my voice according unto thy lovingkindness: O Lord, quicken me according to thy judgment" (Psalm 119: 147-149).

It is as Jeremy Taylor wrote, "Meditation is the tongue of the soul and the language of our spirit."

JESUS AND THE WORD ARE ONE

John wrote, "In the beginning was the Word, and the Word was with God, and the Word was God. The same was in the beginning with God. All things were made by him; and without him was not any thing made that was made. In him was life; and the life was the light of men" (John 1:1-4).

Jesus is at the heart and center of God's Word. Henry H. Halley wrote, "Christ, the center and heart of the Bible, the center and heart of history, is the center and heart of our lives. Our eternal destiny is in His hand." How true this is.

Figures of speech, mainly metaphors and similes, for Jesus are found in every book in the Bible. They let us know how important He is. Here are some types of Christ we find in the Scriptures, and as you look at each, pause and calmly reflect on its meaning. Meditate upon who Jesus is:

1. In Genesis Jesus is the ram at Abraham's altar, involved in the creation, the seed of the woman, and the ark of salvation. He is a King in the line of Judah, typified in Melchizidek, and the suffering servant and rejected brother.
2. In Exodus Jesus is the Passover Lamb, the Deliverer, and the High Priest. He is manna from Heaven, the rock that was struck at Horeb, and the Tabernacle.
3. In Leviticus Jesus is the High Priest, the sacrifice for our sins, and our way of approach to the Father. He is the scapegoat that bore the sins of the people.
4. In Numbers Jesus is the pillar of cloud by day and the pillar of fire by night, the Tabernacle, and the smitten rock out of which living water flows. Jesus is typified in the bronze serpent. He is the King.
5. In Deuteronomy Jesus is the city of our refuge, a prophet like Moses, and the great law giver. He is a prophet who will be worshiped by angels.
6. In Joshua Jesus is the scarlet thread that Rahab hung from her window, the Judge and law giver, and the Deliverer. He is typified in the person of Joshua, the leader into the Promised Land and the commander of the army.

7. In Judges Jesus is our Judge and law giver.
8. In Ruth Jesus is our Kinsman-Redeemer, our lover, and our protector.
9. In First Samuel Jesus is our anointed prophet and priest. He is exalted by God with power.
10. In Second Samuel Jesus is the son of David who is greater than David. He is typified by the lives of David and Jonathan.
11. In the Book of First Kings Jesus is our reigning and perfect King. He is typified in the life of Solomon.
12. In the Book of Second Kings Jesus is the perfect King, the man of God, and the Word of God.
13. In First Chronicles Jesus is the reigning King. He is exalted by God with power. He is typified in Solomon's Temple and the wisdom of Solomon.
14. In Second Chronicles Jesus is the perfect King, priest, and prophet. He is the Rock.
15. In Ezra Jesus is our faithful scribe, the builder and restorer of the Church. He is typified in the person of Zerubbabel, the rebuilder of the Temple.
16. In Nehemiah Jesus is the rebuilder of everything that is broken. The rebuilder of broken walls, governor of the Church, our restorer and protector.

17. In Esther Jesus is Mordecai sitting faithfully at the gate and our Advocate.

18. In Job Jesus is the Redeemer who lives forever. He is the dayspring from on High. He is typified in the suffering of Job and the blessings that would follow.

19. In Psalms Jesus is our Shepherd, the All in all, beloved of God, our Rock, and our fortress. He is the Son of God who will be resurrected.

20. In Proverbs Jesus is our wisdom, the wisdom of God personified. He is from everlasting.

21. In Ecclesiastes Jesus is our wisdom, the Preacher, the Son of David, and the King of Jerusalem.

22. In the Song of Solomon Jesus is the beautiful Bridegroom, the perfect lover, and the King of peace. He is typified in the Bridegroom's love for and marriage to the bride.

23. In Isaiah Jesus is the suffering servant, the Messiah, the Holy One of Israel, the Prince of peace, salvation, righteousness, our comfort, and our Judge. He was born of a virgin. He is Immanuel (God with us). He would have the seven-fold Spirit upon Him. He would heal the blind, the deaf, and the lame and be a light to the Gentiles. He would become a guilt offering for sin.

24. In Jeremiah Jesus is the righteous branch and the Lord, our righteousness. He is typified in the weeping prophet.
25. In Lamentations Jesus is the weeping prophet and the man of sorrows.
26. In Ezekiel Jesus is the four-faced man, the Son of man who was sent to rebellious Israel.
27. In Daniel Jesus is the fourth man in the fiery furnace, the smitten stone that fills the earth, and the King of kings. He is the Son of man who will come in the clouds of Heaven.
28. In Hosea Jesus is love that is forever faithful, the patient bridegroom, and the healer of the backslider. He is typified in Hosea's faithfulness to his adulterous wife.
29. In Joel Jesus is seen baptizing us with the Holy Spirit, and He is our deliverer and judge. He is the Messiah that will offer salvation to all mankind.
30. In Amos Jesus is our burden bearer, the heavenly bridegroom, and our judge.
31. In Obadiah Jesus is our Savior, judge, and the executor of divine retribution.

32. In Jonah Jesus is the foreign missionary who takes the Word of God to the world. He is the One who is greater than Jonah. He is the forgiving God.

33. In Micah Jesus is the messenger with beautiful feet and the rejected King. We learn from this book that He will be born in Bethlehem.

34. In Nahum Jesus is the avenger of the elect, our Stronghold in the day of trouble, and the prophet of comfort and vengeance.

35. In Habakkuk Jesus is the God of our salvation, the Judge of Babylon, and the Rewarder of those who seek Him. He is the great evangelist who is crying for revival. He is typified by Habakkuk, particularly in his role as an intercessor and prayer warrior.

36. In Zephaniah Jesus is the Lord who is mighty to save and the executor of judgment. He is the Restorer of the remnant.

37. In Haggai Jesus is the restorer of our lost heritage, the prophet, priest and King, and the builder of the Lord's house. He is the cleansing fountain.

38. In Zechariah Jesus is our fountain, the righteous branch, Yahweh's servant, the smitten shepherd, and the King-priest. He is the pierced Son.

39. In Malachi Jesus is the Sun of Righteousness who rises with healing in His wings, the Messenger of the New Covenant, the refiner and purifier of His people.

40. In Matthew Jesus is the Christ, the Son of the Living God, the Head of the Church, and the Savior. He is the King of the Jews and the Bridegroom.

41. In Mark Jesus is the great miracle-worker, the suffering servant, and the mighty King. He is the Holy One of God.

42. In Luke Jesus is the Son of man, our sympathetic High Priest, and our Savior. He is the horn of salvation and the consolation of Israel.

43. In John Jesus is the door by which everyone must enter, the Son of God, and the One who brings eternal life. He is the Lamb of God, the bread of life, the light of the world, the I AM, the Good Shepherd, the resurrection and the life, and the true vine.

44. In Acts Jesus is the shining light that appears to Saul on the Road to Damascus, He is the One who is sitting at the right hand of God, and He is the Prince of the Kings of the Earth. He is the ascended Lord, the Prince of life, the Judge of the living and dead, and the hope of Israel.

45. In Romans Jesus is the Justifier, the Lord our righteousness, the Redeemer, and the Savior. He is the Root of Jesse, the Just One, and the baptizer in the Holy Spirit.

46. In First Corinthians Jesus is our Resurrection, the foundation of the Church, the great unifier, the sacrifice for our sins, the resurrected One, and the coming King. He is the first fruits and the last Adam.

47. In Second Corinthians Jesus is our sin bearer, the Son of God, the Reconciler, and the One who anoints.

48. In Galatians Jesus redeems us from the Law and He is the seed of Abraham, and our Liberator. He is the One who sets us free. He is the Lord Jesus Christ.

49. In Ephesians Jesus is portrayed as unsearchable riches. He is our heavenly King, Reconciler, the Head of the Body of Christ, and the Giver of ministry gifts. He is the cornerstone.

50. In Philippians Jesus supplies our every need according to His riches in glory, the source of all fruits of righteousness, the One who humbled himself even though He was equal with God, and the coming One. His is the name that is above all names.

51. In Colossians Jesus is the fullness of the
Godhead bodily, the preeminent One,
and the Redeemer who has the image of
God. He is the image of the invisible God,
the Head of the Body, the beginning, the
firstborn from the dead, and the hope
of glory.

52. In First Thessalonians Jesus is our soon-
coming King and our risen Lord. He is the
Lord of peace.

53. In Second Thessalonians Jesus is our coming
King, great Judge, and the faithful One.

54. In First Timothy Jesus is the Mediator
between God and man, the enabler, God in
the flesh, and the King of kings.

55. In Second Timothy Jesus is the Victor over
death and the resurrected seed of David. He
is the King of ages.

56. In Titus Jesus is the One who appoints
leaders in the Church and our coming Savior.
He is our blessed hope, the great God
and Savior.

57. In Philemon Jesus is a friend that sticks
closer than a brother and He is the
Controller of His servants' destinies. He is
the Lord Jesus Christ.

58. In Hebrews Jesus is the blood of the everlasting covenant, the Son and image of God, the Captain and Author of our salvation, our apostle, and our High Priest. He is the Heir of all things.

59. In James Jesus is the Lord who heals the sick, our unchangeable Father, the wisdom of God, our Husbandman, and our coming Lord. He is the Lord of glory and the Judge at the door.

60. In First Peter Jesus is the Chief Shepherd, the chief cornerstone, and the resurrected One.

61. In Second Peter Jesus is the Savior, the coming One, and our Deliverer.

62. In First John Jesus is the word of life, our Advocate, the propitiator of our sins, and the Messiah. He is love.

63. In Second John Jesus is the Son of God and God in the flesh. He gives eternal life.

64. In Third John Jesus is the Truth, the One who is good. He is righteous.

65. In Jude Jesus is the Lord who will come with 10,000 saints, our Preserver, the coming judge, and the merciful One. He is the only wise God, our Savior.

66. In Revelation Jesus is the Lord of lords, King of kings, the Alpha and Omega, the beginning, the ending, and the great I Am. He is also the coming One, the Son of man, the great Judge, the Lion of Judah, the conquering One, the Lamb of God, the bridegroom, faithful, true, and the Word of God. He is the bright and morning star.

Who is Jesus to you?

MEDITATION UPON GOD'S NAMES

There are more than 600 names of God. I've listed some of them below. Take time to meditate upon each one and let God's light shine through. You will be enlightened and encouraged as you discover who God is to you.

As we take a look at some of the Hebrew names of God in the following list, let's pause and calmly think of each one:

- Adonai—Almighty God, our Sovereign Lord and Ruler.
- El-elyon—The Lord most high—the most-high God.
- El-olam—The everlasting God who is and always will be.

- El-shaddai—The All-sufficient One, who always meets the needs of His people.
- Jehovah-elohim—The eternal Creator of the universe—everyone and everything.
- Jehovah-jireh—The Lord, our Provider—the One who supplies all our needs.
- Jehovah-nissi—The Lord, our banner.
- Jehovah-ropheka—The Lord who heals us.
- Jehovah-shalom—The Lord, our peace.
- Jehovah-Tsidkenu—The Lord, our righteousness.
- Jehovah-mekaddishkem—The Lord, our sanctifier.
- Jehovah-sabaoth—The Lord of hosts.
- Jehovah-shammah—The Lord is present—the ever-present One.
- Jehovah-rohi—The Lord, our Shepherd.
- Jehovah-hoseenu—The Lord, our Maker.
- Jehovah-eloheenu—The Lord, our God.

The names of God help us to understand Him more fully. They show us what God does for us and what He wants to do for us. They reveal His attributes to us and help us to understand Him more fully.

There are several other figures of speech in the

Bible that help us to see His nature more clearly. I've listed some of these for your meditation. Some of these terms apply to the Father, and some apply to Jesus. They reveal His qualities to us and show us how He is always helping us:

- The Branch.
- The chief cornerstone.
- A consuming fire.
- A refuge from the tempest.
- A Father to Israel.
- The great High Priest.
- A man of war.
- A rewarder of all who diligently seek Him.
- A shadow from the heat.
- A shelter.
- A hiding place.
- A rock of refuge.
- A strong tower.
- A sun and shield.
- A sure foundation.
- A very present help in trouble.
- Abba, Father.
- An advocate with the Father.
- Alpha and Omega.

- The ancient of days.
- The author and finisher of our faith.
- The bread of life.
- A mighty buckler.
- The hope of glory.
- The wonderful counselor.
- The dayspring from on high.
- Everlasting Father.
- Father of lights.
- The fountain of living waters.
- The Judge of all.
- The Guide of my youth.
- The Helper of the fatherless.
- I Am That I Am.
- The majesty on high.
- Our shield.
- Our song.
- Our strength and power.
- Our strong rock.
- Our dwelling place.
- The righteous Father.

He is all these things to you and so much more. Our God is the great I Am, and He defines himself as:

- I Am That I Am.
- I am a Father to Israel (and to you).
- I am a great King.
- I am alive forevermore.
- I am Alpha and Omega.
- I am for you.
- I am from above.
- I am God Almighty.
- I am gracious.
- I am He that comforts you.
- I am holy.
- I am married unto you.
- I am merciful.
- I am the God of Abraham, Isaac, and Jacob.
- I am the God of your fathers.
- I am the Lord that sanctifies you, heals you, makes all things, your God, and your exceeding great reward.

Jesus said, "I am. . . "

- He that liveth and was dead.
- The bread of life.
- The door.
- The first and the last.

- The good shepherd.
- The light of the world.
- The living bread.
- The resurrection and the life.
- The root and offspring of David.
- The Son of God.
- The Son of man.
- The vine.
- The way, the truth, and the life.
- With you always.

INTIMACY WITH GOD
THROUGH BIBLE MEDITATION

In the above examples we have shown some of God's attributes and qualities. Who does He want to be to you? He is the God who. . .

- Always makes intercession for you.
- Comforts you in all tribulation.
- Commanded the light to shine out of darkness.
- Crowns you with His loving kindness and tender mercies.
- Daily loads you with benefits.
- Dwells on High.

- Forgives all your iniquities.
- Heals all your diseases.
- Called you into His eternal glory by Christ Jesus.
- Has given you the earnest of the Spirit.
- Lives forever.
- Makes the clouds His chariots.
- Makes His angels spirits and makes His ministers a flaming fire.
- Does wondrous things.
- Quickens all things.
- Redeems your life from destruction.
- Satisfies your mouth with good things.
- Blesses you.
- Helps you.
- Establishes you and keeps you from evil.
- Wills that all people be saved.

His Son, Jesus, Is the One who. . .

- Gave himself as a ransom for you.
- Gave himself for your sins.
- Abolished death.
- Is over all.
- Was delivered for your offenses.

- Is always faithful to Him who appointed Him.
- Was raised for your justification.
- Is the way, the truth, and the life.
- Is before all things.

God wants to have intimacy with you. That's why He created you, and that's why He gave you His Word, which is a book that was written for you. All God's promises are for you to believe, receive, and apply to your life.

By meditating upon God's Word you are letting God know that you believe Him and trust Him, and what father does not want his children to trust and believe him? God is your heavenly Father, and He loves you with an everlasting love.

The Scriptures contain the most anointed words ever written. They are inspired by God. (See 2 Timothy 3:16.) Back in the seventies I attended a church that sang the Scriptures (First Christian Assembly in Plainfield, New Jersey). That was such a wonderful way to worship. As we sang God's Word, we truly were lifted into the heavenlies, and in the process we memorized blessed passages of Scripture.

We would sing some of these choruses over and over again, and our hearts would be filled with the truth of God's Word. I feel so blessed to have had such a rich experience of worship and prayer based entirely on God's Word.

PERSONALIZE GOD'S WORD AS YOU MEDITATE

Make it personal. Use the personal pronouns "I" and "me" when you meditate upon God's Word. Here's an example: "Lord God, thank you for all the promises of your Word. As I confess my sins to you, I know you are faithful to forgive me and to cleanse me from all unrighteousness." (See 1 John 1:9.)

God is thrilled when He hears His Word being personalized and spoken back to Him. It's because He knows the value of these words to set us free, to give us hope, to help us, to conquer temptations, to lead us, to guide us, and to do so many other things for us. Once we understand these things, we will spend much time in the Bible, and we will speak forth its words with conviction and power.

F.B. Meyer wrote, "Devout meditation on the Word is more important to soul-health even than prayer. It is more needful for you to hear God's words than that God should hear yours, though the one will always lead to the other."

Now let's put some of what we've learned to practice through the following meditations that are based completely on the Word of God. May you be richly blessed as you do so.

PART III

---⬡⬡⬡---

BIBLE MEDITATIONS FOR ALL YOUR NEEDS

*Blessed is the man that
walketh not in the counsel of the ungodly,*

*nor standeth in the way of sinners,
nor sitteth in the seat of the scornful.*

*But his delight is in the law of the Lord;
and in his law doth he meditate day
and night.*

*And he shall be like a tree planted by the
rivers of water,*

*that bringeth forth his fruit in his season;
his leaf also shall not wither; and whatsoever
he doeth shall prosper.*

(Psalm 1:1-3)

1
ACCEPTANCE

To the praise of the glory of his grace, wherein he hath made us accepted in the beloved.
(Ephesians 1:6)

Central Focus: You have accepted Jesus Christ as your Savior, and He has accepted you completely. He will always continue His workmanship in your life. He is not finished with you.

Points to Ponder: I accepted Jesus as my Savior, and He accepts me just as I am. This knowledge enables me to accept myself in spite of my weaknesses, failures, and imperfections. I thank God for His love, which removes all fear from me. (See 1 John 4:18.)

Bible Meditation: I fear the Lord, and through His grace I will work righteousness. I know I am accepted by Him, and I am so thankful for His acceptance in my life. To the praise of the glory of His grace, I know I have been accepted in the beloved, and this is a thrilling truth to me. To be accepted by the Lord of glory astounds me and fills me with His love.

I have found grace in the Lord's sight. He has magnified His mercy in my life. He truly has accepted me! He accepts the freewill offerings of my mouth, and He teaches His judgments to me. My goal is to please the Lord Jesus Christ, as I walk by faith and not by sight. I am willing to be absent from the body and to be present with Him. He is my Beloved, and I will remain linked to Him in this life and the life that is to come.

With these thoughts in mind, I will continue to work for the Lord so that whether I am absent or present from my body, I will be accepted by Him, for I know that we must all appear before the judgment seat of Christ. When I appear before Him, I want to hear those powerful words, "Well done, thou good and faithful servant."

The Father has blessed me with every spiritual blessing in heavenly places in Christ. He has chosen me in Him before the foundation of the world, that I would be holy and blameless before Him in love. He has predestinated me unto adoption into His family, according to the good pleasure of His will. This is what I want as well.

I choose to abide in the Lord and to let His words abide in me. By so doing, I know that what I ask of Him will be accomplished. I want to be a fruitful disciple of Jesus. I will keep His commandments and abide in His love. As a result, I know that my joy shall be full. To abide in Jesus is to abide in love, peace, and joy every day.

With His help I will love others in the same way He has loved me and accepted me. What a friend I have in Jesus. I did not choose Him, but He chose me and ordained me, that I would bring forth much fruit and that my fruit would remain. He is a friend that sticks closer than any brother.

God has chosen me, and He considers me to be precious. As a living stone, I am being built up into a spiritual house. The Lord is so precious to me. I believe in Him.

Scriptures: Acts 10:35; Ephesians 1:6; Genesis 19:19-21; Psalm 119:108; 2 Corinthians 5:6-10; Matthew 25:21; Ephesians 1:3-5; John 15:7-16; Proverbs 18:24; 1 Peter 2:5.

A Bible Prayer About Acceptance: Father, thank you for accepting me in the beloved and for bringing me to your banqueting table. Your banner over me is love, and I rejoice in you. In your acceptance I find my reason for being and I find great peace. In Jesus' name, Amen.

A Word of Wisdom: *"God loves each of us as if there were only one of us"* (Augustine).

2

ANSWERED PRAYER

❧

I will hasten my word to perform it.
(Jeremiah 1:12)

Central Focus: God hears and answers prayer. He wants us to present our needs to Him. He is always there for us.

Points to Ponder: So much is accomplished through prayer. I know that God hears and answers my prayers. In fact, He knows what I have need of even before I express it to Him through prayer. (See Matthew 6:8.) Prayer truly changes things; most of all it changes me!

Bible Meditation: When I pray to God, I know He hears me and He will answer me. I have set my love upon Him, and He has delivered me and He knows my name. When I call upon Him, He will answer me. He will be with me in times of trouble and He will satisfy me with long life and show me His salvation.

He hears my prayers, and He answers my prayers in His perfect timing.

He will answer me even before I call, and while I am yet speaking He will hear me. God hearkens to me when I call to Him. When I call unto Him, He answers me and shows me great and mighty things that I never knew. My Father knows what my needs are even before I pray, but He wants me to express my needs to Him.

As I ask, I know it shall be given to me. As I seek, I know I will find. As I knock, I know that it shall be opened unto me. Whatever I ask for in prayer, believing, I shall receive. Jesus promises, "Whatsoever ye shall ask in my name, that will I do, that the Father may be glorified in the Son. If ye shall ask any thing in my name, I will do it" (John 14:13–14). Praise the Lord for these wonderful prayer promises from God's Word!

I will abide in Jesus, and I will let His words abide in me. As I do so, I will ask what I will, and I know it shall be done unto me. I will ask and receive, that my joy may be full, as Jesus promised. The joy that Jesus gives to me is so wonderful.

I have this confidence in the Lord, that if I ask anything according to His will, I know He hears me, and I know that I have the petitions that I have desired. To pray according to His will, I now realize, is to pray according to His Word.

I am so blessed! I choose never to walk in the counsel of the ungodly nor stand in the path of sinners. Nor will I ever sit in the seat of the scornful. My delight is in the Word of God, and I will meditate upon God's Word day and night. In so doing I know I shall become like a tree planted by the rivers of water that brings forth its fruit in its season. As a result of meditating upon God's Word, I know that whatever I do shall prosper.

Scriptures: Job 22:27; Psalm 91:14-16; Psalm 18:31; Isaiah 65:24; Jeremiah 29:12; Jeremiah 33:3; Matthew 6:8; Matthew 7:7-8; Matthew 21:22; John 14:13-14; John 15:7; John 16:23-24; 1 John 5:14-15; Psalm 1:1-3.

A Bible Prayer About Answered Prayer: Heavenly Father, I know you hear me when I pray. Thank you for teaching me to pray without ceasing and to give thanks to you. Through your grace I will abide in Christ and let His words abide in me, and I know that through this you will answer my prayers. Thank you, Father.

A Word of Wisdom: *"He wishes to give who advises us to ask"* (Augustine).

3

ARMOR OF GOD

Put on the whole armor of God, that ye may be able to stand against the wiles of the devil.
(Ephesians 6:11)

Central Focus: By putting on the whole armor of God, you are fully equipped for spiritual warfare, because God provides you with all the offensive and defensive weapons you will ever need.

Points to Ponder: The armor of God is impenetrable, and that's why I must put it on every day. It protects my mind, my heart, and every part of me. It enables me to quench all the fiery darts of the wicked one. By wearing His armor I am able to be strong in the Lord and in the power of His might. (See Ephesians 6:10.)

Bible Meditation: God has provided me with HIs impenetrable armor to protect me from the evil one. I will be strong in the Lord and in the power of His might. I will put on the whole armor of God, and in so doing, I will be able to stand against all the wiles of the devil. Greater is He that is within me than he who is in the world.

It is clear to me that I do not wrestle against flesh and blood, but against principalities, powers, the rulers of the darkness of this world, and spiritual wickedness in high places. Because this is true, I will take unto me the whole armor of God. This will enable me to stand in the evil day and, having done all, to stand, having my loins girt about with truth and wearing the breastplate of righteousness.

My feet will be shod with the preparation of the gospel of peace. I take hold of the shield of faith with which I will be able to quench all the fiery darts of the wicked one. I put on the helmet of salvation and the sword of the Spirit, which is the Word of God. I will pray always with all prayer and supplication in the Spirit, and watch thereunto with all perseverance and supplication for all saints.

I cast off the works of darkness, and I put on the armor of light that God has given to me. With God's help I will walk honestly, as in the day, not in rioting, drunkenness, chambering, wantonness, strife, and envying. Instead, I will put on the Lord Jesus Christ, and I will make no provision for my flesh, to fulfill its lusts.

God is strengthening me according to His Word. He is my strength, and His Word is a lamp unto my feet and a light unto my path. God is my rock, my fortress, my deliverer, and my strength. He is my buckler and my high tower. I will call upon Him, for He is worthy to be praised, and so shall I be saved from my enemies.

God has girded me with strength and He is making my way perfect. He has made my feet like the feet of a hind, and He has set me upon high places. He is teaching my hands to war, so that a bow of steel can be broken by my arms. He has given me the shield of salvation, and His right hand is holding me up.

His mighty power is within me, upon me, and surrounding me.

I am so thankful for the protective armor that God has given to me. I will ever praise Him and His holy name.

Scriptures: Ephesians 6:10-18; 1 John 4:4; Romans 13:12-14; Psalm 27:14; Psalm 119:28; Psalm 18:1-3; Psalm 18:32-35; Psalm 18:46-50.

A Bible Prayer About the Armor of God: Dear God, thank you for the armor you've provided for me. I will wear it each day, for I know this will enable me to stand effectively against all the wiles of the devil. My loins are girt about with the spirit of truth, and my heart is protected by the breastplate of righteousness. My feet are shod with the preparation of the gospel of peace. Above all, I am taking the shield of faith whereby I am able to quench all the fiery darts of the wicked one. The helmet of salvation is protecting my mind, and I wield the sword of the Spirit, which is your mighty Word. Father, thank you so much for giving me your armor to protect me during spiritual warfare.

A Word of Wisdom: *"God is not a deceiver, that He should offer to support us, and then, when we lean upon Him, should slip away from us"* (Augustine).

4
ASSURANCE

❦

And the work of righteousness shall be peace;
and the effect of righteousness quietness
and assurance forever.
(Isaiah 32:17)

Central Focus: To be assured means to be confident, secure, and fully persuaded. God offers this kind of assurance to every believer.

Points to Ponder: Assurance is a sense of certainty and confidence. The assurance that Christ has given to me is, as Fanny Crosby wrote, a blessed assurance. I am assured that God loves me and His promises assure me that He will do everything He says. All of His promises are Yes and Amen through Christ Jesus. (See 2 Corinthians 1:20.)

Bible Meditation: I draw near to my Abba-Father with a true heart in the full assurance of faith. My heart has been sprinkled from an evil conscience and my body washed with pure water. God's righteousness is at work in my life, and it provides me with peace, quietness, and assurance forever. Blessed assurance. Jesus is mine!

The Resurrection of Jesus Christ gives my heart a wonderful sense of assurance. My heart is comforted as it is being knit together with other believers in love and unto all riches of the full assurance of understanding, to the acknowledgment of the mystery of God, the Father, and Jesus Christ in whom are hid all the treasures of wisdom and knowledge. This is true assurance.

The Gospel of Jesus Christ came to me in power, in the Holy Spirit, and in much assurance. I am now a follower of Jesus Christ, and I have great joy in the Holy Spirit. It is my desire to show great diligence to the full assurance of hope until the end. I will not be slothful. Instead, I will be a follower of them who through faith and patience inherit the promises of God.

God has given me great boldness to enter into the holiest by the blood of Jesus, by a new and living way, which He consecrated for me. I will hold fast the profession of my faith without wavering. God is so faithful to me, and I stand upon His promises, which are found in His Word. Through these, He has assured me of His love and blessings. This is the kind of assurance that everyone is searching for.

The Word of God is my source of assurance. It was given by the inspiration of God, and it is profitable for doctrine, reproof, correction, and instruction in righteousness. Through God's Word it is possible for me to be made whole, one who is thoroughly furnished unto all good works.

I am so thankful that I am assured of abundant and eternal life, and this life has already begun!

Scriptures: Hebrews 10:22; Isaiah 32:17–28; Acts 17:31; Colossians 2:2–3; 1 Thessalonians 1:5; Hebrews 6:11–12; Hebrews 10:19–20; 2 Timothy 3:14–17.

A Bible Prayer About Assurance: Lord God, thank you for the assurance you have given to me deep within my heart. It is an assurance of salvation, deliverance, eternal life, victory, joy, and so many other wonderful things that you have given to me. Your grace assures me that I will always have all that I need, including your love, protection, and truth.

A Word of Wisdom: *"An infinite God can give all of himself to each of His children. He does not distribute himself that each may have a part, but to each one He gives all of himself as fully as if there were no others"* (A.W. Tozer).

5

BLESSINGS

❧

Blessed be the God and Father of our Lord Jesus Christ, who hath blessed us with all spiritual blessings in heavenly places in Christ (Ephesians 1:3)

Central Focus: God loves to bless His children with every good and perfect gift. These are already yours through Christ Jesus, the Lord.

Points to Ponder: I am already blessed in every spiritual way. (See Ephesians 1:3.) I do not have to ask God for wisdom, strength, victory, hope, love, or anything else, because He has already provided these spiritual amenities to me. I will count my blessings and name them one by one. Hallelujah, I am blessed indeed.

Bible Meditation: God has already blessed me with every spiritual blessing in heavenly places in Christ. His blessings are upon my head. His blessing prospers me, and He adds no sorrow with it.

As I learn to hearken to His voice and obey Him, His blessings will come on me and overtake me. Praise His holy name! He is blessing me in the city and in the field. He is blessing the fruit of my body and the fruit of my fields. He is blessing my basket and my store. Truly His blessings are surrounding me and filling me up.

I am blessed as I come in and as I go out. God is smiting my enemies, and He is commanding His blessing upon my storehouse and upon all that I set my hand to do. He is blessing me in the land that He has given to me.

As I learn how to be a faithful person as He is, I know I will abound with blessings. The truth is that I already do abound with blessings, and I am so thankful to my heavenly Father for all He has done for me. As I take time to meditate upon the blessings He has given to me, my heart overflows with thanksgiving.

I place all my trust in the Lord and, as I do so, I am greatly blessed. I will trust in Him with all my heart and not lean upon my own understanding. In all my ways I will acknowledge Him, and I know He will direct my steps.

I will ever make the Lord my trust, for I know He will always bless me. I will listen for the Lord's voice and I will wait at His door. In so doing I know I will be blessed. I have found Him as my Savior and Lord, and I have found life in Him. His favor is upon me.

He feeds me with the finest of wheat and satisfies me with honey from the rock. I will never forget all the Lord's blessings and benefits to me. He forgives all my sins and heals my diseases. He has redeemed my life from the pit and He has satisfied me with good things. My youth is being restored like the eagle's.

As I meditate upon God's Word both day and night, I will be careful to do what it says. This assures me that I will be both prosperous and successful. I will not forget the Lord's teaching. I will keep His commands in my heart, and I know my years will be prolonged and He will bless me with prosperity.

I am so very blessed!

Scriptures: Ephesians 1:3; Proverbs 10:6; Proverbs 10:22; Deuteronomy 28:1-9; Psalm 2:12; Proverbs 3:5-6; Proverbs 8:32-35; Psalm 81:16; Psalm 103:2; Joshua 1:8; Proverbs 3:1.

A Bible Prayer About Blessings: Father, your blessings truly overwhelm me. I'm blessed coming in and going out. I am truly blessed, and I know you daily load me with benefits. Thank you, Lord, for all the blessings I have received, am receiving, and will receive from your hands. I will focus on your blessings in my life instead of any issues I may be facing.

A Word of Wisdom: *"You can see God from anywhere if your mind is set to love and obey Him"* (A.W. Tozer).

6
COMMITMENT

❧

Commit thy way unto the Lord; trust also in him; and he shall bring it to pass.
(Psalm 37:5)

Central Focus: Commitment is a choice; it is an act of your will. God wants you to commit your life and way unto Him, for He is totally committed to you. He wants you to succeed, and your commitment to Him is a key to your success.

Points to Ponder: A commitment is a binding promise. God is totally committed to you. Are you totally committed to Him? The Bible says, "Nevertheless I am not ashamed: for I know whom I have believed, and am persuaded that he is able to keep that which I have committed unto him against that day" (2 Timothy 1:12).

Bible Meditation: Through God's grace I will trust in Him completely. I know He will help me to do good and to dwell in the land He has given to me. I will delight in Him, and I know He will give me the desires of my heart.

I commit my way to the Lord, and I know He will bring good things to pass in my life. I rest in Him and wait patiently upon Him. I will not worry about evildoers who seem to prosper. Help me to cease from anger and to forsake wrath.

I will never be ashamed of my relationship with the Lord. I know Him in whom I have believed, and I am persuaded that He is able to keep that which I've committed unto Him against that day.

The Lord has sanctified me through the truth. His Word is truth. By committing whatever I do to the Lord, I know my plans will succeed. Hallelujah! I make that commitment now.

The sacrifices of God are a broken spirit. He will not despise a broken and contrite heart. My desire is to be broken before Him. Because of God's wonderful mercies to me, I present my body to Him as a living sacrifice, holy and acceptable unto Him, for this is my reasonable service.

I will not be conformed to this world. Instead, I will be transformed by the renewing of my mind, that I may prove what God's good, acceptable, and perfect will is.

I will keep that which is committed to my trust, and I will avoid vain and profane babblings and the so-called opposition of science, which some professing have erred from the faith.

I realize that in a little while the wicked will no longer be. The meek will inherit the Earth and shall delight themselves in the abundance of peace. Through the Lord's help I will walk in meekness always.

Through God's grace I will use my mouth and tongue to speak only wisdom. I will keep God's Word within my heart, so I will speak His truth to others. I commit my life to waiting on, serving, honoring, and worshipping the Lord.

Scriptures: Psalm 37; 2 Timothy 1:12; Romans 12:1–2; 1 Timothy 6:20–21.

A Bible Prayer About Commitment: Abba–Father, thank you so much for adopting me into your family. I know you are eternally committed to me and that you want only good for me. This knowledge makes me commit my life unto you, and I ask that your grace would enable me to remain committed unto you at all times. In Jesus' name I pray, Amen.

A Word of Wisdom: *"That is why He warned people to 'count the cost' before becoming Christians. 'Make no mistake,' He says, 'if you let me, I will make you perfect. The moment you put yourself in my hands, that is what you are in for. Nothing less, or other than that'"* (C.S. Lewis).

7

COMPASSION

❧

But thou, O Lord, art a God full of compassion, and gracious, long suffering, and plenteous in mercy and truth. O turn unto me, and have mercy upon me; give thy strength unto thy servant.
(Psalm 86:15-16)

Central Focus: In order to be a follower of God, we must be compassionate, which means we are full of love and mercy toward our fellowmen. Compassion comes from the ability to understand and have empathy for what another is going through.

Points to Ponder: God's compassion never fails. He loves us with an everlasting love. By walking in His compassion we are able to feel what others feel and to share in bearing their burdens. Paul wrote, "Bear ye one another's burdens, and so fulfill the law of Christ" (Galatians 6:2).

Bible Meditation: I want to be an imitator of God. Therefore, I will have compassion for my fellow human beings and I will love my fellow believers. I will always endeavor to be courteous to others. Instead of rendering evil for evil, I will bless others, because I know I have been called to inherit God's blessing.

God is full of compassion. He is gracious, patient, and plenteous in mercy and truth. He is giving me His strength, His mercy, and His compassion. He is showing me how to be compassionate toward others.

My Father has forgiven me of all my iniquities. His works are so great, and His work is honorable and glorious. His righteousness endures forever. I will remember His wonderful works and the truth that He is gracious and full of compassion, and I will try to emulate these qualities in my own life.

I highly respect the Lord, and I take delight in His commandments. His promise is that His seed will be mighty upon the Earth, and the generation of the upright shall be blessed. He is the light that shines in the darkness.

With God's help I will always show favor and generosity toward others, and I will handle all my affairs with discretion. I will let God's compassion flow through me to other people.

I will speak of the glorious honor of God's majesty and all His wonderful works. Through His grace I will follow His example in everything. I want to be gracious and full of compassion. Therefore, I will be slow to anger and of great mercy as He is. His tender mercies are over all His works, and all His works shall bless Him.

I will speak of the glory of His kingdom and I will talk to others about His great power. He will help me as I do so. He will uphold me when I fall.

I want to be united with my fellow-believers, to show compassion toward them, to love them as members of my family, and to always be full of mercy toward them. My goal will to be a blessing to others.

I will abide in the Lord, for I know this will keep me from sin and all deception. I will strive to be righteous and compassionate as He always is. Through His grace I will build myself up in His love, and I will continually look for the mercy of the Lord Jesus Christ unto eternal life. I will make a difference in society by practicing compassion wherever it is needed.

My God is able to keep me from falling and to present me faultless before His presence with exceeding joy. He is the only wise God, my Savior, and I give Him glory, majesty, dominion, and power both now and forevermore.

Scriptures: 1 Peter 3:8-9; Psalm 86:15-16; Deuteronomy 13:17; Psalm 78:38; Psalm 111:2-4; Psalm 112:1-5; Psalm 145:6-14; 1 Peter 3: 8-9; Jude 22-25.

A Bible Prayer About Compassion: Dear God, you are my compassionate Father, and I want to be like you. Help me to show compassion to all I come in contact with. Help me to share your compassion with others. I love you with all my heart.

A Word of Wisdom: *"Compassion is the basis for all morality"* (Arthur Schopenhauer).

8
CONFIDENCE

❦

*For the Lord shall be thy confidence, and shall
keep thy foot from being taken.*
(Proverbs 3:26)

Central Focus: As you confide in God, your
confidence in Him will grow, and you will be
assured that He will take care of you.

Points to Ponder: Confidence connotes strength
and certainty, and both of these qualities stem
from faith. Self-confidence is built as we learn to
walk in faith. Solomon wrote, "For the Lord shall
be thy confidence, and shall keep thy foot from
being taken" (Proverbs 3:26).

Bible Meditation: In the fear of the Lord there is
strong confidence, and to fear Him is to respect,
honor, and love Him. The fear of the Lord is a
fountain of life that enables me to escape from
the devil's snares.

With the Lord's help I will preach the Kingdom
of God and teach those things that concern the
Lord Jesus Christ. I will do so with all confidence,
because I love Him so.

It is my desire to make all people see what is

the fellowship of the mystery, which from the beginning of the world has been hid in God, who created all things by Jesus Christ. I want the Church to know about the principalities and powers in the heavenly places. I want my fellow-believers to experience the manifold wisdom of God, according to the eternal purpose, which He purposed in Jesus Christ, my Lord, in whom I have boldness and access with confidence by the faith I have in Him.

God has made me a partaker with Christ. Therefore, I will hold on to the confidence that He gives to me to the very end. I have in Heaven a better and enduring substance than anything I know here. Therefore, I will never cast away my confidence, which has great recompense of reward. I will practice patience so that after I have done the will of God, I will receive the promise He has extended to me.

I will abide in the Lord so that when He appears, I will have confidence and not be ashamed before Him at His coming. There is therefore now no condemnation in my life. My heart does not condemn me. God is greater than my heart and He knows all things. I have great confidence in and through Him.

This promise gives me great confidence: "And

whatsoever we ask, we receive of him, because we keep his commandments, and do those things that are pleasing in his sight. And this is his commandment: That we should believe on the name of his son Jesus Christ, and love one another, as he gave us commandment. And he that keepeth his commandments dwelleth in him, and he in him. And hereby we know that he abideth in us, by the Spirit which he hath given us" (1 John 3:22-24).

And this is the confidence I have in Him, that, if I ask anything according to His will, he hears me. And if I know that He hears me and has heard what I've asked for, I know that I have the petitions that I have desired of Him. This confidence comes to me as I meditate upon His Word, for His Word reveals His will to me and provides me with all the confidence I need.

Scriptures: Proverbs 14:26-27; Acts 28:31; Ephesians 3:9-12; Hebrews 3:14; Hebrews 10:35; 1 John 2:28; Romans 8:1; 1 John 3:20-22; 1 John 3: 23-24; 1 John 5:14-15.

A Bible Prayer About Confidence: Father, I put all my confidence and trust in you, and, as I do so, my sense of self-confidence grows. I realize that all my confidence comes from you, and this helps me to understand that you and I can face anything together. Thank you for giving me your confidence and strength.

A Word of Wisdom: *"Confidence is preparation. Everything else is beyond your control"* (Richard Kline).

9

CONTENTMENT

❧

But godliness with contentment is great gain.
(1 Timothy 6:6)

Central Focus: Contentment comes when we place our trust in God and enter His rest.

Points to Ponder: Real contentment involves thinking of yesterday without regret and tomorrow without fear. It as the Apostle Paul said, "Not that I speak in respect of want: for I have learned, in whatsoever state I am, therewith to be content" (Philippians 4:11).

Bible Meditation: God has taught me not to speak in terms of my wants. I am so thankful that He has taught me to be content in whatever state I find myself. I know how to be abased, and I know how to abound. Praise His holy name! Everywhere and in all things I am instructed both to be full and to be hungry, both to abound and to suffer need.

Indeed, I can do all things through Christ who strengthens me, and this assures me that contentment will be mine. I know that I brought nothing into this world, and it is certain that I will carry nothing out. Therefore, having food and clothing, I shall be content.

Realizing that the love of money is the root of all evil, I will flee from its influence in my life along with other worldly things, and I will follow after righteousness, godliness, faith, love, patience, meekness. I will fight the good fight of faith and lay hold on eternal life.

As I seek contentment, I will let my conversation be without covetousness in any form, and I will be content with such things as I have, for I know that my Lord will never leave nor forsake me. In this knowledge I find the key to contentment.

The Lord is my helper, and I will not fear what others can do to me. Contentment comes when I reflect on the fact that Jesus Christ is the same today, yesterday, and forever. Hallelujah!

The Comforter, who is the Holy Ghost, whom the Father has sent in the name of Jesus, will teach me all things and bring to my remembrance whatever Jesus has said and the Word of God proclaims. Jesus has given me His peace, but not as the world gives. Because I know this is true, I will not let my heart be troubled and I will reject any temptation toward discontentment that might come my way.

I know my God will supply all my need according to His riches in glory by Christ Jesus. Therefore, I will walk worthy of the Lord unto all pleasing, being fruitful in every good work, and increasing in the knowledge of God. He strengthens me with all might, according to His glorious power, unto all patience and longsuffering with joyfulness.

For these reasons I give thanks unto the Father who has made me a partaker of the inheritance of the saints in light. This is true contentment. Indeed, He has delivered me from the power of darkness and has translated me into the Kingdom of His dear Son. In Him I have redemption through His blood and the forgiveness of sins.

I thank God that I am a truly contented person.

Scriptures: Philippians 4:11; Philippians 4:12-13; 1 Timothy 6:5; 1 Timothy 6:10-12; Hebrews 13:5-8; John 14:26-27; Philippians 4:19; Colossians 1:10-14.

A Bible Prayer About Contentment: Almighty God, I rest in you. Your supernatural peace that surpasses all understanding helps me to stay focused on the things that are important in my life. It brings great contentment to my heart when I realize who you are to me and all you've done for me. Thank you, Father.

A Word of Wisdom: *"We tend to forget that happiness doesn't come as a result of getting* *something we don't have, but rather of recognizing and appreciating what we do have"* (Frederick Keonig).

10
COURAGE

❦

Be strong and of a good courage, fear not,
nor be afraid of them: for the Lord thy God,
he it is that doth go with thee;
he will not fail thee, nor forsake thee.
(Deuteronomy 31:6)

Central Focus: When we choose not to fear, we are filled with courage, and it is courage that leads us to go forth against all opposition. It encourages us and gives us strength when we act upon our courage and walk away from fear.

Points to Ponder: Charlotte Gray wrote, "Disasters sweep the world—war and disease, earthquake and flood and fire—but always in their wake come acts of courage and concern that astound the human heart. Light in utter darkness." "Only be thou strong and very courageous, that thou mayest observe to do according to all the law, which Moses my servant commanded thee: turn not from it to the right hand or to the left, that thou mayest prosper whithersoever thou goest" (Joshua 1:7).

Bible Meditation: With God's help I will be strong and of good courage. I will not fear, because I know God is with me forever. Hallelujah! He will not fail me nor forsake me. Therefore, I will not fear and I will not allow myself to become dismayed.

Like Joshua, I will be strong and of good courage. I will obey the Lord. I will keep on keeping on, and I will not turn to the left or the right, so that I will prosper in whatever I do. The Word of God shall not depart from my mouth. I will meditate upon its precepts day and night that I may always do all that is written therein. The result, I know, will be that my way shall be prosperous wherever I go and God will give me good success.

As I wait on the Lord, I know I shall have great courage, because He is strengthening my heart, and He is fighting my battles for me. Through the encouragement He imparts to me, He strengthens my heart. This causes me to hope in Him.

I will use the courage God gives to me to encourage others. I will be very courageous to keep and do all that God's Word declares, and I will cleave to the Lord. I realize that I, as one person, can chase a thousand, for God fights for me. I love Him so much.

God is helping me to be courageous and valiant. I will not be afraid nor dismayed, for I know the Lord my God will always help me. He will fight my battles for me and with me. It is God that girds me with strength and courage. He lights my candle and enlightens my darkness. By Him I have run through a troop and leaped over a wall. His way is perfect, and His Word is tried. He is a buckler to all those who trust in Him.

He teaches my hands to war. He has given me the shield of His salvation, and His right hand holds me up. His gentleness has made me great. He has enlarged my steps under me, so that my feet will not slip. I have pursued my enemies and overtaken them.

My Father has girded me with strength and courage. He has subdued under me those who have risen against me. The Lord lives! Blessed be my rock. I will let the God of my salvation be exalted. God avenges me and subdues my enemies. He delivers me.

Therefore, I give thanks to Him, and I will sing praises to His name. I am so very thankful for His deliverance and mercy in my life. He makes me courageous.

Scriptures: Deuteronomy 31:6; Joshua 1:6-9; Psalm 27:14; Psalm 31:24; Isaiah 41:6-7; Joshua 23:6-8; 2 Samuel 13:28; 2 Chronicles 32:7-8; Psalm 18:28-50.

A Bible Prayer About Courage: Dear God, I am encouraging myself in you, as David did. Thank you for encouraging my heart and keeping me above all discouragement. I will go forth in your courage and strength, and I know this will be enough for me. Thank you for enabling me to be strong and courageous through you. Hallelujah!

A Word of Wisdom: *"All serious daring starts from within"* (Eudora Welty).

11
DELIVERANCE

❧

*The angel of the Lord encampeth round about
them that fear him, and delivereth them.*
(Psalm 34:7)

Central Focus: God brings deliverance to all
captives who love Him—those who are enslaved
in any way—and His promise is there for us to
appropriate. He will deliver the godly from all
temptations. (See 2 Peter 2:9.)

Points to Ponder: God is a mighty Deliverer. He
tears down strongholds that are erected by
the enemy. There is nothing that is too hard for
Him. "I will love thee, O Lord, my strength. The
Lord is my rock, and my fortress, and my deliverer;
my God, my strength, in whom I will trust; my
buckler, and the horn of my salvation, and my
high tower" (Psalm 18:1–2).

Bible Meditation: Whenever I cry out to the Lord,
He hears me, and He always delivers me from
all troubles. He delivers my soul from death and
keeps me alive during times of famine. God is high
above all the Earth, and He is exalted above all
gods. He preserves my soul and delivers me out
of the hands of the wicked.

I realize that treasures of wickedness profit nothing, but righteousness delivers me from death. I will love the Lord, my strength. He is my rock and my fortress. He is my Deliverer and my God. He is my strength in whom I will trust. He is my buckler, the horn of my salvation, and my high tower.

I will call upon the Lord who is worthy to be praised, and so shall I be saved from all enemies. The Lord be magnified. Even though I am poor and needy, He thinks about me, for He is my help and my deliverer. He will not tarry when it comes to helping me.

God will make haste to help me. He is my help and my deliverer. I put my trust in the Lord, and I know He will never let me be confused. He delivers me in His righteousness and causes me to escape. Hallelujah! He inclines His ear to me and saves me.

He is my strong habitation, and it is thrilling to know that I can go to Him at any time. He is my rock and my fortress. He is delivering me out of the hand of the wicked, for He is my hope and my trust from my youth.

The Lord is my strength, and He teaches my hands to war and my fingers to fight. He is my goodness and my fortress. He is my high tower and my deliverer. He is my shield, and I put all my trust in Him. He subdues my enemies under me.

The Lord drew me out of many waters. He delivered me from my strong enemy and from all those who hated me. They opposed me in the time of my calamity, but the Lord was my stay. He brought me forth into a large place and delivered me because He takes delight in me.

God is my helper. He is ever with me. I will praise His name, for it is good. He has delivered me out of all trouble. Praise His holy name!

The Lord is teaching His way to me, and I will walk in His truth. He is uniting my heart to fear His name. I will praise Him with all my heart, and I will glorify His name forevermore. Great is His mercy toward me. He has delivered my soul from the deepest hell.

I love the Lord because He has heard my voice and my supplications. He has inclined His ear unto me. Therefore, I will call upon Him as long as I live. When I called upon Him, He delivered my soul out of many troubles. He is gracious and merciful. He has delivered my soul from death, my eyes from tears, and my feet from falling.

I will walk before Him in the land of the living. Praise the Lord!

Scriptures: Psalm 34:17; Psalm 34:19; Psalm 97:10; Psalm 18:1-3; Psalm 40:16-17; Psalm 70:5; Psalm 71:1-2; Psalm 71:3-5; Psalm 144:1-2; Psalm 18:16-19; Psalm 54:7; Psalm 86:11-17; Psalm 116.

A Bible Prayer About Deliverance: Mighty Deliverer, you have lifted me above all fear and temptation. This is true deliverance. I will no longer fear others or anything, because you are my light and my salvation. You are my strength. Thank you, Father.

A Word of Wisdom: *"The wise man in the storm prays to God, not for safety from danger, but for deliverance from fear. It is the storm within which endangers him, not the storm without"* (Ralph Waldo Emerson).

12

ENCOURAGEMENT

✧

*And David was greatly distressed; for the
people spake of stoning him, because the
soul of all the people was grieved, every man
for his sons and for his daughters: but David
encouraged himself in the Lord his God.*
(1 Samuel 30:6)

Central Focus: When we encourage others, we
plant seeds of courage in their hearts. When we
encourage ourselves in the Lord, our faith grows.

Points to Ponder: We are called to be encouragers.
In this role and ministry, we impart courage to the
heart of someone who is discouraged. God had
done so with us. The ministry of encouragement is
so important, for it brings life to others. Strengthen
others through your prayers, bless others with the
love of God, and encourage others with the hope
you find in the God of all hope.

Bible Meditation: As I wait upon the Lord, I know
He is encouraging me and strengthening my
heart. He is strengthening me and encouraging
me through His Word. I have chosen the way of
truth and His testimonies are ever before me.

I cast all my care upon the Lord, for I know He

cares for me. I will be sober and vigilant, because my adversary, the devil, as a roaring lion, walks about seeking whom he may devour. I will resist him as one who is steadfast in the faith, knowing that the God of all grace, who has called me unto His eternal glory by Christ Jesus is perfecting, establishing, strengthening, encouraging, and settling me.

I will praise the Lord with my whole heart. I will worship toward His holy temple and praise His name for His loving-kindness and for His truth, for He has magnified His Word above his name. When I cry unto God, He always strengthens and encourages me.

I will be of good courage as the Lord strengthens my heart and encourages my spirit. All of my hope is in Him. God is granting me, according to the riches of His glory, that I would be strengthened with might in my inner man. Christ will dwell in my heart by faith, and I will be rooted and grounded in love. In this way I will be able to comprehend with all saints what is the breadth, length, depth, and height of His matchless love. God has enabled me to know the love of Christ, which surpasses all knowledge, and I am being filled with all the fullness of Him. Praise the Lord!

I will live my life unto Him who is able to do

exceeding abundantly above all that I ask or think, according to the power that works within me. Unto Him be glory in the Church by Christ Jesus throughout all ages, world without end.

With the Lord's help I will walk worthy of Him unto all pleasing, being fruitful in every good work and increasing in the knowledge of Him. He is strengthening me with all might, according to His glorious power, unto all patience and longsuffering with joyfulness. This is true encouragement to me.

God is encouraging me, and I know that I can do all things through Christ who strengthens me, and my God is supplying all my need according to His riches in glory by Christ Jesus. I will give thanks to the Lord, and I will be strong in Him and in the power of His might.

I am greatly encouraged as I put on the whole armor of God, because I know this will enable me to stand against all the devil's wiles. There is no encouragement that can compare to the encouragement that God has given to me.

Scriptures: Psalm 27:14; Psalm 119:28–29; 1 Peter 5:7–10; Psalm 138:1–3; Psalm 31:24; Ephesians 3:16–19; Ephesians 3:20–21; Colossians 1:10–11; Philippians 4:13; Philippians 4:19; Ephesians 6:10–11.

A Bible Prayer About Encouragement: Through

your strength, Father God, I will be an encourager. Thank you for encouraging me and giving me the desire to encourage others. Lead me in the ministry of encouragement and give me empathy and compassion for others.

A Word of Wisdom: *"If you have made mistakes, there is always another chance for you. You may have a fresh start any moment you choose, for the thing we call 'failure' is not the falling down, but the staying down"* (Mary Pickford).

13

FAITH

❦

*Let us draw near with a true heart in full
assurance of faith, having our hearts
sprinkled from an evil conscience,
and our bodies washed with pure water.*
(Hebrews 10:22)

Central Focus: Faith enables us to see into the invisible, spiritual realms, and through faith we are able to rise above the circumstances of life. The eye of faith beholds the truth, and the hand of faith appropriates God's promises. Faith comes from God's Word and through faith we are able to overcome the world.

Points to Ponder: The world says, "Seeing is believing," but the believer says, "Believing is seeing." God says, "Faith is the substance of things hoped for, the evidence of things not seen" (Hebrews 11:1). Walking in faith is walking in confidence, security, and love.

Bible Meditation: Faith is the substance of things hoped for, and the evidence of things not seen. Through faith I am able to understand that the worlds were framed by the Word of God, so that things which are seen were not made of things which do appear.

Without faith it is impossible to please God, for all who come to God must believe that He is and that He is a rewarder of all those who diligently seek Him. Through faith I will diligently seek Him. I look unto the Author and Finisher of my faith, the Lord Jesus, because He is so faithful to me.

Even though I've never seen Him, I love Him, and I rejoice with unspeakable joy that is full of glory. Through Christ I believe fully in God who raised Jesus from the dead and gave Him glory. All my faith and hope are in Him.

I thank God that I've been born again, for whatsoever is born of God overcomes the world, and the victory that truly overcomes the world is faith. It was by grace through faith that I was saved, and that was not as a result of anything I did; it was the gift of God, not of works.

Christ dwells in my heart by faith. As I put on the whole armor of God, I lift up the shield of faith by which I shall quench all the fiery darts of the wicked one. Through His grace I will continue in the faith, grounded and settled. I will not be moved away from the hope of the gospel.

As I have received Christ Jesus the Lord, I will walk in Him, rooted and built up in Him and established in the faith. This causes me to abound with thanksgiving. Faith in Christ, not the works of the Law, has justified me.

I am crucified with Christ; nevertheless, I live. However, it is not I, but Christ, who lives within me, and the life which I now live in the flesh I live by the faith of the Son of God who loved me and gave himself for me. Praise His holy name!

I choose to be filled with the Holy Spirit and to bear His fruit in all the relationships and responsibilities of my life: love, joy, peace, longsuffering, gentleness, goodness, faith, meekness, and temperance. Against such there is no law.

I walk in the peace of God and love with faith. I will be watchful as I stand fast in the faith, and I will be strong in the Lord. I will walk by faith and not by sight. Having been justified by faith, I now have peace with God through the Lord Jesus Christ. It is by Him that I have access into the grace wherein I stand, and I rejoice in the hope of the glory of God.

Scriptures: Hebrews 11:1-2; Hebrews 11:6; Hebrews 12:2; 1 Peter 1:8; 1 Peter 1:21; 1 John 5:4; Ephesians 2:8-9; Ephesians 3:17; Colossians 1:23; Colossians 2:6-7; Galatians 2:16; Galatians 2:20; Galatians 5:22-23; Ephesians 6:23; 1 Corinthians 16:13;

2 Corinthians 5:7; Romans 5:1-2.

A Bible Prayer About Faith: Dear Lord, help my unbelief. I want always to walk in faith and trust. Through your grace I will trust in you with all my heart and lean not upon my own understanding. In all my ways I will acknowledge you, and I know you will always direct my steps. Praise your mighty name!

A Word of Wisdom: *"Faith is to believe what you do not see; the reward of this faith is to see what you believe"* (Augustine).

14
FELLOWSHIP

∾∾

But if we walk in the light, as he is in the light,
we have fellowship one with another,
and the blood of Jesus Christ his Son
cleanseth us from all sin.
(1 John 1:7)

Central Focus: Fellowship is a strengthening factor in our lives. Our fellowship with the Father and the Son empowers us and our fellowship with other believers helps to keep us from wandering away and getting off track.

Points to Ponder: The Bible says, "Can two walk together, except they be agreed?" (Amos 3:3). True fellowship results in unity of heart and mind, and Jesus prayed that we would be one as He and the Father are one. Let us walk together in agreement, fellowship, and unity.

Bible Meditation: The early believers loved to have fellowship with each other. They were steadfast in the apostles' doctrine, fellowship, breaking of bread, and prayer. I want to be like them. God is so faithful to me, and He has called me unto the fellowship of His Son, Jesus Christ my Lord. As I fellowship with my Lord and Savior, I am drawn closer to Him, and this helps me to preserve unity with my fellow-believers, that there would be no divisions among us. I will do my part to be perfectly joined with them in the same mind and the same judgment under the Lord's guidance.

Through God's grace I will not allow myself to ever be yoked together with unbelievers, because I know that righteousness and unrighteousness have no fellowship with each other. I am the temple of the living God. He dwells within me. He is my God, and I am one of His company of believers. For this reason I will come out from among those who are worldly, separating myself from them, and I will not touch the unclean thing.

It is my desire to preach the unsearchable riches of Christ and to make all people see what is the fellowship of the mystery, which from the beginning of the world has been hid in God who created all things by Jesus Christ. I will have no fellowship with the unfruitful works of darkness. Rather, I shall reprove them.

If there be any consolation in Christ, if any comfort of love, if any fellowship of the Spirit, and any mercies, I will always endeavor to be likeminded with other believers, having the same love, and being of one accord and one mind. This is true fellowship. I will not let anything be done through strife or vainglory, but in lowliness of mind, I will esteem others as being better than myself.

My goal is to know Jesus Christ ever more intimately and to know the power of His resurrection and the fellowship of His sufferings, being made conformable unto His death, if, by any means, I might attain to the resurrection of the dead.

I press toward the mark for the prize of the high calling of God in Christ Jesus. I will declare that which I have seen and heard to others, that I might have fellowship with them. Truly my fellowship is with the Father and with His Son, Jesus Christ.

God is light and in Him there is no darkness at all. I will walk in His light, as He is in the light. I will have fellowship with other believers, realizing that the blood of Jesus Christ cleanses me from all sin. Hallelujah!

Scriptures: Acts 2:42; 1 Corinthians 1:9-10; 1 Corinthians 6:14-17; Ephesians 3:8-9; Ephesians 5:11; Philippians 2:1-3; Philippians 3:10; Philippians 3:14; 1 John 1:5-7.

A Bible Prayer About Fellowship: Father, thank you for wanting to have fellowship with me. My fellowship truly is with you, with your Son, Jesus Christ, and with my fellow-believers. Help me to remember the importance of maintaining each of these lines of fellowship in my life, for I know I will be greatly strengthened as I do so.

A Word of Wisdom: *"Continual meditation on the Word is not ineffectual. . . . God, by one and another promise, establishes our faith"* *(John Calvin).*

15
FINANCIAL SECURITY

⚜

*But my God shall supply all your need
according to his riches in glory by Christ Jesus.*
(Philippians 4:19)

Central Focus: Security of any kind is found in God alone. He is our financial security, and He loves to give to His children. Everything we are and have belongs to Him, and we must place all financial issues in His hands.

Points to Ponder: To be financially secure we must follow God's ways, and this means that we are always to put Him first in our lives, to practice good stewardship, and to realize that everything we are and have is His.

Bible Meditation: Nothing is too hard for God. He will supply all my need according to His riches in glory by Christ Jesus. My heavenly Father is helping me with every financial problem in my life. He is my strength and He is my security.

When I allow Him to have first place in my life and when I seek His kingdom and His righteousness first, He will add all things unto me. Praise His holy name! As I learn to tithe my income and give to God and His people, God will open the windows of Heaven and pour down a blessing until I have no more needs.

The Lord is my Shepherd. Therefore, I shall not want. His plans for me are for my welfare and not for evil in any form. He has given me a future and a hope.

God is teaching me to give, and I want to be like Him. He is the Giver of every good and perfect gift. I will remember His promise that good measure, pressed down, shaken together, and running over will be given to me. I know that I will be blessed with the same measure that I give.

I will be a faithful steward over all God has given to me. I will not lay up treasures upon Earth, but in Heaven. No longer will I earn wages to put into a bag with holes.

I know I cannot serve both God and mammon, for any attempt to do so will result in me loving one and hating the other. I want my priorities to be in their proper order at all times.

I will not let God's Word depart from my mouth, but I will meditate upon it both day and night. With His help I will observe to do all that is written therein. Then I know He will make my way prosperous and give me good success.

God owns everything, including everything

that I have. Every beast of the forest is His and so are the cattle on a thousand hills. All the fowls of the mountains and the wild beasts of the field are His. Indeed, the world is His, the world in all its fullness.

For this reason (and so many others) I offer my vows of thanksgiving to Him and I call upon Him. I know He will deliver me from all financial struggles and difficulties. It is in this certainty that I find my security.

Scriptures: Jeremiah 32:27; Philippians 4:19; Matthew 6:33; Malachi 3:8–10; Psalm 22:1; Jeremiah 29:11; James 1:17; Luke 6:38; Haggai 1:6; Matthew 6:19–21; Psalm 50:10–15.

A Bible Prayer About Financial Security: O Most High God, it gives me a great sense of peace to know that you have provided financial security for me and mine. I will not worry about anything, for I know you will take care of me. In fact, I cast all my care upon you, for I know you care deeply about me.

A Word of Wisdom: *"We can only learn to know ourselves and do what we can, namely, surrender our will and fulfill God's will in us"* (St. Teresa of Avila).

16

FORGIVENESS

❧

If we confess our sins, he is faithful and just
to forgive us our sins, and to
cleanse us from all unrighteousness.
(1 John 1:9)

Central Focus: Because God forgives us, we are able to forgive others. Indeed, forgiveness is the only solution to many of the issues we face with other people. It is as we experience God's forgiveness, that we are enabled to forgive others.

Points to Ponder: Whenever someone wrongs me, I have a choice to either forgive them or be angry and hold an unending grudge against them. The former choice is the pathway to freedom, whereas the latter choice is the pathway to bitterness. The Bible says, "Looking diligently lest any man fail of the grace of God; lest any root of bitterness springing up trouble you, and thereby many be defiled" (Hebrews 12:15). Notice that a person who holds bitterness and unforgiveness within defiles others along with himself.

Bible Meditation: Because I have confessed my sins to Him, I know God has forgiven me. The blood of Jesus Christ cleanses me from all sin—

past, present, and future. I am so thankful for the forgiveness that the Lord extends to me. I wait for Him, and in His Word I do hope.

My loving God has opened my eyes, turned me from darkness to light and from the power of Satan unto the power of God so that I would receive His forgiveness and His wonderful inheritance. He has sanctified me by faith. Hallelujah!

Blessed be the God and Father of my Lord Jesus Christ who has blessed me with all spiritual blessings in heavenly places in Christ. According as He has chosen me in Him before the foundation of the world, that I would be holy and without blame before Him in love.

He predestinated me to be adopted into His family by Jesus Christ, according to the good pleasure of His will, to the praise of the glory of His grace, wherein He has made me accepted in the beloved. Through the blood of Christ I have redemption and the forgiveness of sins according to the riches of His grace.

I give thanks to the Father who has made me a partaker of the inheritance of the saints in light. He has delivered me from the power of darkness and has translated me into the Kingdom of His dear Son in whom I have redemption through

His blood, even the forgiveness of sins. Praise the Lord!

I will let no corrupt communication proceed from my mouth. I will speak edifying words that will minister grace to the hearers. I will not grieve the Holy Spirit, for I realize that it is by Him that I've been sealed unto the day of redemption. I will not permit bitterness, wrath, anger, clamor, and evil speaking to be a part of my life. I will put these things, along with all malice, away from me.

It is my heart's desire to be kind to others, tender-hearted, and forgiving, even as God for Christ's sake has forgiven me. I will be a follower of God and walk in love, as Christ also has loved me and has given himself as an offering and sacrifice to God.

I lift up my soul to the Lord, for I know He is so good and He is always ready to forgive my sins. He is plenteous in mercy to me. He gives heed to my prayers and He attends to the voice of my supplications. Hallelujah!

Scriptures: 1 John 1:9; 1 John 1:7; Psalm 130:4-5; Acts 26:18; Ephesians 1:4-7; Colossians 1:12-14; Ephesians 4:29-5:1.

A Bible Prayer About Forgiveness: Heavenly Father, thank you so much for forgiving me of my sins. Help me to forgive others in the same way you have forgiven me. Help me, also, to forgive myself. I am so glad to know that all my sins are buried in the depths of the deepest sea and you will not remember them anymore. Praise God!

A Word of Wisdom: *"Each of us has a soul, but we forget to value it. We don't remember that we are creatures made in the image of God. We don't understand the great secrets hidden inside of us"* (St. Teresa of Avila).

17

FREEDOM

❧

And ye shall know the truth,
and the truth shall make you free.
(John 8:32)

Central Focus: The Lord Jesus died to set us free from sin, self, and Satan. In Him we are free indeed. We must, therefore, stand fast in the liberty wherewith Christ has made us free.

Points to Ponder: There is a difference between truth and facts. Facts are changeable, but the truth is fixed and permanent. It is the truth that sets us free and enables us to experience the glorious liberty of the sons of God. (See Romans 8:21.)

Bible Meditation: Jesus Christ is the way, the truth, and the life, and through Him I find spiritual freedom that is too wonderful to describe. Because Jesus has set me free I know I am free indeed. Hallelujah!

Having been made free from sin, I have now become a servant of righteousness. I yield all of my life and every part of my body to serve righteousness unto holiness. There is therefore no condemnation to me because I am in Christ Jesus and I walk not after the flesh but after the Spirit, for the law of the Spirit of life in Christ Jesus has set me free from the law of sin and death.

I will stand fast in the liberty wherewith Christ has made me free, and I will never be entangled again with any yoke of bondage. I will keep the law of God forever, and I will walk at liberty, for I seek His precepts.

The Spirit of the Lord is upon me, and the Lord has anointed me to preach good tidings unto the meek, and He has sent me to bind up the broken-hearted, to proclaim liberty to the captives, and the opening of the prison to them that are bound. What a glorious ministry this is!

God has delivered me from the bondage of corruption, and I have entered into the glorious liberty of the sons of God. Now the Lord is the Spirit, and where the Spirit of the Lord is there is liberty. I will walk in His liberty each step of the way.

God has called me to liberty, and I will never use my liberty for an occasion for the flesh, but by love I will serve others, for I know that all the law is fulfilled in this: to love my neighbor as myself. The spiritual freedom that God has imparted to me impels me to do so.

I will walk in the Spirit, for I know that this will

keep me from fulfilling the lusts of my flesh. With God's help I will keep on looking into the perfect law of liberty. I will not be a forgetful hearer. Instead, I shall be a doer of God's Word. I know God will bless me. Hallelujah!

With well doing I will put to silence the ignorance of foolish people. I will walk in freedom, and I will not use my liberty in any malicious way. It is my heart's desire to ever be a servant of God. Through God's grace I will honor all others, love the brotherhood, fear God, and honor those in authority over me.

God has called me to follow in the steps of Christ. I will learn from His example and endeavor to do what I know He would do. He did no sin, and no guile could be found within Him. He has enabled me to be dead to sin and to be alive to righteousness, for by His stripes I've been healed.

According to Christ's divine power He has given unto me all things that pertain to life and godliness, including spiritual freedom. He has given me so many great and precious promises, that by these I would be a partaker of the divine nature, having escaped the world and all its lusts.

I am free from the fear of the future and free from the guilt of the past. Hallelujah!

Scriptures: John 14:6; John 8:32; John 8:36; Romans 6:18-19; Romans 8:1-2; Galatians 5:1; Romans 8:21; 2 Corinthians 3:17; Galatians 5:13-16; 1 Peter 2:15-17; 1 Peter 2:21-24; 2 Peter 1:3-4.

A Bible Prayer About Freedom: Father, thank you for giving me a spiritual sense of freedom that truly sets me free. Because I know your Son, Jesus Christ, I am free indeed. Thank you for Him and for the freedom that He brings to me. Through your power and your grace I will stand fast in the liberty whereby Christ has set me free, and I will not ever be entangled again with any yoke of bondage.

A Word of Wisdom: *"Prayer is the wing wherewith the soul flies to Heaven and meditation the eye wherewith we see God"* (Ambrose).

18
FRUITFULNESS

⚜

I am the vine, ye are the branches:
He that abideth in me, and I in him,
the same bringeth forth much fruit:
for without me ye can do nothing.
(John 15:5)

Central Focus: God wants us to bear good fruit for Him, so He has given His Holy Spirit to us. We should ask Him each day to refill us with the Holy Spirit so that we will produce His fruit in all the relationships and responsibilities of our lives. The fruit of the Spirit consists of love, joy, peace, patience, gentleness, goodness, faith, meekness, and temperance. Bearing fruit for Him can also mean leading others to Jesus Christ.

Points to Ponder: Meditating upon God's Word leads to fruitfulness in our lives, as Psalm 1 points out: "But his delight is in the law of the Lord; and in his law doth he meditate day and night. And he shall be like a tree planted by the rivers of water, that bringeth forth his fruit in his season; his leaf also shall not wither; and whatsoever he doeth shall prosper" (Psalm 1: 2–3). As we learn to abide in Jesus and let His Word abide in us, we will be fruitful in every good way.

Bible Meditation: Jesus is the vine and His Father is the husbandman. Every branch in Him that does not bear fruit he takes away, and every branch that does bear fruit, He purges so that it will bring forth more fruit. I am clean through the Word He has spoken unto me.

I will abide in Jesus and I know He will abide in me. As the branch cannot bear fruit by itself, except it abide in the vine, neither can I bear fruit unless I abide in Christ. He is the vine, and I am but a branch. As I learn to abide in Him, I will bear much fruit, and this is what I want. Without Him I can do nothing.

As I learn to abide in Him and let His words abide in me, I know that He will give me what I ask of Him. Praise the Lord for this wonderful promise!

God is filling me with the knowledge of His will in all wisdom and spiritual understanding so that I might walk worthy of Him unto all pleasing, being fruitful in every good work, and increasing in the knowledge of Him. He is strengthening me with all might, according to His glorious power, unto all patience and longsuffering with joyfulness.

I give thanks to the Father who has caused me to partake of His inheritance with the saints in light. He has delivered me from the power of darkness and has translated me into the kingdom of His Son in whom I have redemption through His blood, even the forgiveness of sins.

When God chastens me, I know the result will yield the peaceable fruit of righteousness in my life. Through Jesus I will offer the sacrifice of praise to God continually, that is, the fruit of my lips, and I will give thanks unto His name.

With God's help I will walk in the wisdom that comes from above, which is pure, peaceable, gentle, and easy to be entreated. This wisdom is full of mercy and good fruits, and without hypocrisy. It shows no partiality. I will remember that the fruit of righteousness is sown in peace of them that make peace. Through God's grace I will be a peacemaker at all times.

Scriptures: John 15:1-7; Colossians 1:10-12; Hebrews 12:11; Hebrews 13:15; James 3:17-18.

A Bible Prayer About Fruitfulness: Heavenly Father, Jesus said that we will be known by our fruits. Help me to be a fruit-bearing Christian at all times. I did not choose you, but you chose me. Thank you, Lord. Help me ever to remember that you have chosen me and ordained me to bring forth fruit. I pray that my fruit would remain; I praise you for your promise that whatever I ask of you in the name of Jesus, you will give to me. In Jesus' name, Amen.

A Word of Wisdom: *"Whatever engages my attention when I should be meditating on God . . . does injury to my soul"* (A.W. Tozer).

19
GENTLENESS

❦

And the servant of the Lord must not strive;
but be gentle unto all men, apt to teach,
patient, in meekness instructing those that
oppose themselves.
(2 Timothy 2: 24-25)

Central Focus: Gentleness is a fruit of the Holy Spirit in our lives. It is a quality that endears us to others, and it leads to good works.

Points to Ponder: To be gentle is to be merciful, graceful, faithful, meek, and respectful toward others. Billy Graham said, "The word gentle was rarely heard before the Christian era, and the word gentleman was not known. This high quality of character was a direct by-product of Christian faith."

Bible Meditation: God is enabling me to be ready for every good work. With His continuing help I will speak evil of no one. Instead, I shall be gentle, showing meekness toward all others. I thank God for the kindness and love that He showed by sending the Savior to the Earth. It is not by works of righteousness that I have done, but according to His mercy, that He saved me.

According to His mercy He saved me by the washing of regeneration and the renewing of the Holy Ghost, which He shed on me abundantly through Jesus Christ, my Savior. Hallelujah! I am so thankful that I have been justified by His grace, that I should become an heir according to the hope of eternal life.

For all these wonderful reasons I will walk in gentleness and I will be careful to maintain good works. It is by the meekness and gentleness of Christ that I am able to have any gentleness at all. Though I walk in the flesh, I do not war after the flesh. I realize that the weapons of my warfare are not carnal, but they are mighty through God to the pulling down of strongholds.

The Holy Spirit within me quickens me. He fills my life with love, peace, joy, patience, meekness, gentleness, faithfulness, goodness, and self-control. I now belong to the Lord Jesus Christ, and He is helping me crucify my flesh with all its affections and lusts. I will live and walk in the Spirit for the rest of my life.

To be gentle makes me happy, for I know God's promise that the meek shall inherit the Earth. Meekness is not weakness, but it stems from wisdom. I want to be wise and understanding toward all people and to show by my good behavior the gentleness of wisdom.

As a gentle person, I will not use flattering words. I will not covet or seek glory from others. Instead, I want to be like the Apostle Paul who was gentle among the believers, as a nursing mother cherishes her own children.

Gentleness produces beauty in my life. This beauty does not come from outward adornment but from my inner self, the unfading beauty of a meek and quiet spirit. This is what I want to show to the world at all times. In God's sight such qualities are of great worth.

I will let the mind of Christ be within me. He, being in the form of God, thought it not robbery to be equal with God. However, He made himself of no reputation and took upon Him the form of a servant and was made in the likeness of mankind. This is the kind of gentleness that I want to show forth to others.

I will take His yoke upon me and learn of Him, for His yoke is easy and His burden is light. His gentleness toward me causes me to want to be gentle toward others.

Scriptures: Titus 3:1–8; 2 Corinthians 10:2–4; Romans 8:11; Galatians 5:22–25; Matthew 5:5; James 3:13–14; 1 Thessalonians 2:5–7; Philippians

2:5-7; Matthew 11:29-30.

A Bible Prayer About Gentleness: "Create in me that warmth of mercy that shall enable others to find thy strength for their weakness, thy peace for their strife, thy joy for their sorrow, thy love for their hatred, thy compassion for their weakness. In thine own strong name I pray, Amen" (Peter Marshall). Father, thank you for your gentleness which has made me great. Help me to walk in gentleness from this day forth.

A Word of Wisdom: *"Nothing is won by force. I choose to be gentle. If I raise my voice may it be only in praise. If I clench my fist, may it be only in prayer. If I make a demand, may it be only of myself"* (Max Lucado).

20
GLADNESS

❦

Thou hast put gladness in my heart,
more than in the time that their
corn and their wine increased.
(Psalm 4:7)

Central Focus: To know Jesus is to be glad, happy, and joyous. As I walk with God, I am filled with gladness.

Points to Ponder: Gladness is characterized by feelings of pleasure or joy. It is a form of happiness. The Lord has put gladness in our hearts so that we will be able to serve Him with gladness and impart His joy to others.

Bible Meditation: God has turned my mourning into dancing for me and He has girded me with gladness. My soul will ever sing unto Him and be joyful. I will give thanks to Him forever.

I love righteousness. How I thank God that He has anointed me with the oil of gladness above all others. Because He is purging me, I know I shall be clean. He is washing me and making me whiter than snow. He is making me to hear joy and gladness. He is creating in me a clean heart and renewing a right spirit within me.

It is my honor to serve the Lord with gladness and to come before His presence with singing. He is the God who made me, and I am a sheep in His pasture. Therefore, I will enter His gates with thanksgiving and go into His courts with praise. I will ever be thankful unto Him and bless His name. He is good and His mercy is everlasting. His truth endures to all generations.

Gladness gives me great hope. The way of the Lord is strength to me. God has imparted everlasting joy and gladness to me, and He has removed all sorrow and sighing from me. I will praise the Lord with my whole heart. I will show forth all of His marvelous works.

I will be glad and rejoice in Him. I will sing praise to the name of the Most High God. I will bless the Lord, who has given me counsel. I have set Him always before me. Because He is at my right hand, I shall not be moved. Therefore, my heart is glad and my soul rejoices. My flesh rests in hope. He has shown me the path of life. In His presence there is fullness of joy, and at His right hand there are pleasures forevermore. Hallelujah!

I will be glad in the Lord and rejoice. I will shout for joy. I will bless the Lord at all times. My soul shall make her boast in the Lord. The humble shall hear thereof and be glad. I will magnify the Lord, and I will exalt His name.

I sought the Lord and he heard me and delivered me from all my fears. When I look unto Him, I am enlightened and my face is not ashamed. His angels encamp around me and deliver me. Hallelujah! Trusting in Him gives me great happiness and joy. It fills me with gladness.

I will ever trust in Him and do good, so I shall live in the land and be fed. I will delight myself in the Lord, and I know He will give me the desires of my heart. Praise His holy name! As I commit my way to Him and trust in Him, I know He will give me the things I've desired of Him.

Scriptures: Psalm 30:11-12; Psalm 45:7; Psalm 51:7-10; Psalm 100; Proverbs 10:28-29; Isaiah 35:10; Psalm 9:1-2; Psalm 16:7-11; Psalm 32:11; Psalm 34:1-8.

A Bible Prayer About Gladness: Heavenly Father, I am so happy in you. Thank you for filling my heart with gladness and gratitude. I feel privileged to be your child and your servant. You have anointed me with gladness. You have restored unto me the joy of my salvation. In your presence there is fullness of joy, and at your right hand there are pleasures forevermore. I want to experience your presence every moment of my life. In Jesus' name, Amen.

A Word of Wisdom: *"There is not in the world a kind of life more sweet and delightful than that of a continual conversation with God"* (Brother Lawrence).

21
GOODNESS

✦

The king shall joy in thy strength, O Lord;
and in thy salvation how greatly shall he
rejoice! Thou hast given him his heart's desire,
and hast not withholden the request
of his lips. Selah. For thou preventest him
with the blessings of goodness: thou settest a
crown of pure gold on his head.
He asked life of thee, and thou gavest it him,
even length of days for ever and ever.
(Psalm 21:1–4)

Central Focus: The word *good* stems from the word God. He is true goodness, and we need Him in order to practice goodness in our lives.

Points to Ponder: God is so good to us, and He shares His goodness with us. It is important to remember that the word *good* is a euphemism for God. There can be no true goodness without Him, because He is goodness. Goodness is a part of the fruit of the Holy Spirit. When we are filled with Him, we are filled with goodness—a wonderful quality that we should always be showing forth.

Bible Meditation: The Lord is my shepherd; I shall not want. He makes me lie down in green pastures, and He leads me beside the still waters. He restores my soul and leads me in the paths of righteousness for His name's sake. Yea, though I walk through the valley of the shadow of death, I will fear no evil, for He is with me and His rod and staff bring comfort to me. He prepares a table before me in the presence of my enemies. He anoints my head with oil. My cup overflows. Surely goodness and mercy shall follow me all the days of my life, and I will dwell in the house of the Lord forever.

The Lord is teaching me His way, and He is leading me in a plain path. I would have fainted had I not seen the goodness of the Lord in the land of the living. Praise God! I will wait on the Lord and be of good courage. As I do so, I know He will strengthen my heart.

How great is the goodness of God, which He has laid up for all who fear Him. He will hide me in the secret place of His presence. Blessed is the Lord. He has shown me His marvelous kindness. I will be of good courage, for I know He is strengthening my heart.

The Word of the Lord is right, and all His works are done in truth. He loves righteousness and judgment. The Earth is full of the goodness of the Lord. The goodness of God endures continually. Oh, that men would praise the Lord for His goodness and for His wonderful works to the children of men. He satisfies the longing soul and fills the hungry soul with goodness.

Blessed be the Lord, my strength. He teaches my hands to war and my fingers to fight. He is my goodness, my high tower, my deliverer, and my shield. I trust completely in Him. The Lord's goodness is great and beautiful.

It is the goodness of God that leads me to repentance. He is the God of hope and He is filling me with all joy and peace in believing, that I may abound in hope through the power of the Holy Spirit. Because of this, I know I am filled with goodness and knowledge which enable me to admonish others in the right way.

God has filled me with His Holy Spirit, and I am now bearing His fruit in my life: love, joy, peace, patience, gentleness, goodness, faith, meekness, and temperance. I am thankful that against these things there is no law. The fruit of the Spirit is in all goodness, righteousness, and truth.

Through His grace, I believe God is counting me worthy of His calling, and thereby I will fulfill all the good pleasure of His goodness and the work of faith with power. In this way I know the name of the Lord Jesus Christ will be glorified in me, and I will be glorified in Him, according to the grace of God and the Lord Jesus Christ.

Scriptures: Psalm 23; Psalm 27:11-14; Psalm 31:19-24; Psalm 33:4-5; Psalm 52:1; Psalm 107:8-9; Psalm 144:1-2; Zechariah 9:17; Romans 2:4; Romans 15:13-14; Galatians 5:22-23; Ephesians 5:6-10.

A Bible Prayer About Goodness: Thank you for your goodness, O God. Your goodness is so great, and your goodness to me has been so wonderful. Help me to never be overcome by evil, but to overcome evil with good. Thank you for giving me a merry heart, because I know that a merry heart does good like a medicine. With your help, I will walk in goodness at all times and I will rejoice in your great goodness to me. Thank you so much, good Father, for being the Giver of every good and perfect gift.

A Word of Wisdom: *"Goodness is love in action, love with its hand to the plow, love with the burden on its back, love following His footsteps who went about continually doing good"* (James Hamilton).

22
GRACE

~≋~

Being justified freely by his grace through the
redemption that is in Christ Jesus.
(Romans 3:24)

Central Focus: God's grace is sufficient for me. His grace keeps me from falling and helps me in every moment of every day. I do not merit His grace, but He freely bestows it upon me.

Points to Ponder: Grace enables me to do what I could not do, to believe what I could not believe, and to become what I could not become— in my own strength. It is God's unmerited favor at work in my life. It is by grace that I am saved, and it is by grace that I am justified, redeemed, and set free. I thank God for His amazing grace that is at work in my life.

Bible Meditation: Sin will never have dominion over me, because I am not under the law, but under grace. The wages of sin is death, but the gift of God is eternal life through Jesus Christ. This is true grace.

I am so thankful for God's grace, which has been given to me by Jesus Christ. In Him I am enriched in all utterance and in all knowledge. By His grace I am what I am, and He did not bestow His grace upon me in vain. It thrills me to know that the abundant grace of God might through the thanksgiving of many redound to the glory of God.

God is able to make all grace abound toward me, that I would have all sufficiency in all things and that I may abound to every good work. This is my desire, and I know it's God's desire for me as well. Indeed, His grace is sufficient for me, and His strength is made perfect in my weakness.

It was by grace that I was saved through faith. This was not of myself and it was not of works. It was the gift of God to me. Hallelujah! I am His workmanship, and I was created unto good works, which God ordained that I should walk in.

God and His Son, the Lord Jesus Christ, loves me and He has given me everlasting consolation and good hope through grace. Therefore, I am able to comfort my heart, as He establishes me in every good word and work.

Through His grace, God has not given me the spirit of fear but of power, love, and a sound mind. Therefore, I am not ashamed of the testimony of the Lord, but I am privileged to be a partaker of the affliction of the gospel according to the power of God.

He saved me and called me with a holy calling, not according to my own works but according to His own purpose and grace, which were given in Christ Jesus before the world began. I will be strong in the grace that is in Christ Jesus.

It's not by works of righteousness which I have done, but according to His mercy that I've been saved by the washing of regeneration and the renewing of the Holy Spirit, which He shed abundantly upon me through Jesus Christ, my Savior. I was justified by His grace, and I became an heir according to the hope of eternal life.

Our High Priest, the Lord Jesus, was tempted in all the same points I have been, yet He was without sin. Knowing this, I am enabled to go boldly before the throne of grace, that I may obtain mercy and find grace to help in my time of need.

It is my desire to be a good steward of the manifold grace of God. I humble myself under God's mighty hand, that He may exalt me in due time. I will cast all my care upon Him, for He cares for me. I will be sober and vigilant, because I know that my adversary, the devil, as a roaring lion, walks about, seeking whom he may devour. However, the God of all grace, who has called me unto His eternal glory by Christ Jesus is perfecting, establishing, strengthening, and settling me. To Him be glory and dominion forever and ever. Amen.

Scriptures: Romans 6:14, 23; 1 Corinthians 1:5; 1 Corinthians 15:10; 2 Corinthians 4:15; 2 Corinthians 9:8; 2 Corinthians 12:9; Galatians 3:8-9; 2 Timothy 1:7-8; 2 Timothy 2:1; Titus 3:5-7; Hebrews 4:15-16; 1 Peter 4:10; 1 Peter 5:7-11.

A Bible Prayer About Grace: God of all grace, I love you and I thank you for saving me, delivering me, and giving me your grace to enable me. Help me to grow in grace and in the knowledge of my Lord and Savior, Jesus Christ. I know I do not deserve your grace, but it is your grace that opens the door for me to have fellowship with you. Thank you for your wonderful grace that is at work in my life. In Jesus' name I pray, Amen.

A Word of Wisdom: *"There is no place like the feet of Jesus for resolving the problems that perplex our hearts"* (G.B. Duncan).

23
GUIDANCE

❧

*I will instruct thee and teach thee
in the way which thou shalt go:
I will guide thee with mine eye.*
(Psalm 32:8)

Central Focus: God guides me each step of my way. He will be my Guide until my death.

Points to Ponder: God guides us in a variety of ways. Some forms of His guidance include the Bible, other believers, the voice of the Holy Spirit, and the inner witness of peace. We need His guidance in our lives, and should pray for it every day. The Bible says, "Trust in the Lord with all thine heart; and lean not unto thine own understanding. In all thy ways acknowledge him, and he shall direct thy paths" (Proverbs 3:5–6).

Bible Meditation: Good and upright is the Lord. He will teach me and show me the way in which I should walk. As I practice meekness, I know He will guide me in judgment and teach me His way. All the paths of the Lord are mercy and truth.

I place all my trust in the Lord God. He will never let me be ashamed, and He will deliver me in His righteousness. He will bow down His ear to me, and He will be my strong rock and a house of defense to save me. Indeed, He is my rock and my fortress. For His name's sake I know He will lead me and guide me.

He is my hiding place. He shall preserve me from trouble. He will compass me about with songs of deliverance. I am so thankful that He is instructing and teaching me. He is leading me in the way in which I should go. He is guiding me with His eye. I will be glad in Him and shout for joy for His guidance in my life.

He is my God forever and ever, and He will be my guide even unto death. Hallelujah! He is holding me with His right hand, and He is guiding me with His counsel. Afterward, He will receive me into glory. God's Word is a lamp unto my feet and a light unto my path. I will walk in the light it sheds each step of my way.

I desire to walk in integrity, for I know that my integrity will guide me. It thrills me to know that the Lord is guiding me continually. He satisfies my soul in drought, and I shall be like a watered garden whose waters never fail. My Father is the guide of my life from my youth on.

God has given light to me. I no longer sit in darkness or in the shadow of death. He is guiding my feet in the way of peace. Hallelujah! The Spirit of truth is guiding me into all truth, and the truth is making me free.

God is guiding me through His Word, His Spirit, other believers, and prayer. Blessed be His holy name!

Scriptures: Psalm 25:8-10; Psalm 31:1-3; Psalm 32:7-11; Psalm 48:14; Psalm 73:23-24; Psalm 119:105; Proverbs 11:3; Isaiah 58:11; Jeremiah 3:4; Luke 1:79; John 16:13; John 8:32.

A Bible Prayer About Guidance: Father, thank you for leading and guiding me. Where you lead me I will follow. I thank you for your Word, which shows me the way to walk. I will walk in your Word, your love, your power, and your grace. Guide me with your eye as I walk hand in hand with you. In Jesus' name, Amen.

A Word of Wisdom: *"Devout meditation on the Word is more important to soul-health even than prayer. It is more needful for you to hear God's words than that God should hear yours, though the one will always lead to the other"* (F. B. Meyer).

24
HAPPINESS

❧

Blessed is every one that feareth the Lord;
that walketh in his ways. For thou shalt eat
the labour of thine hands: happy shalt
thou be, and it shall be well with thee.
(Psalm 128:1–2)

Central Focus: Happiness comes from the multiple blessings of God in my life.

Points to Ponder: To be blessed is to be happy, and we must remember that we are greatly blessed in so many ways. Let's take time to focus on our blessings and, as we do so, we will experience happiness from the Lord. Happiness is a state of being that stems from joy, pleasure, and a feeling of cheerfulness. To be happy we must stay close to Jesus. He said, "These things have I spoken unto you, that my joy might remain in you, and that your joy might be full" (John 15:11).

Bible Meditation: As Job stated, "Happy is the man whom God correcteth: therefore despise not thou the chastening of the Almighty" (Job 5:17). I am thankful for God's correction and guidance in my life, because He always helps me to stay on the right track.

I honor, revere, and respect my Father–God, and it is my desire to walk in all His ways. As I do so, I know I will be happy and it shall be well with me. The Word of God states, "Happy is that people whose God is the Lord" (Psalm 144:15). I am happy in the knowledge that I am a part of that company of people, for God truly is my Lord.

I will sing praise unto my God while I have my being. I will put all my trust in Him, not in other people. I am happy because I have the God of Jacob as my helper and all my hope is in the Lord, my God. Hallelujah! He made Heaven and Earth, the sea, and all that exists. He opens the eyes of the blind and raises up all who are bowed down. He loves the righteous. He shall reign forever unto all generations. Praise the Lord!

I am happy to know the wisdom of God, which He has imparted to me. He has given me spiritual understanding. These wonderful blessings (wisdom and understanding) are a tree of life to me, and it gives me great happiness to know that I will keep on growing as I walk in wisdom.

I will remember the poor and have mercy upon them. As I do so, I know I will experience the happiness of the Lord. Trusting fully in the Lord brings great happiness to me. Where there is no vision the people perish, but those who keep

God's law shall always be happy. I will trust in the Lord, flow with His vision, and experience His happiness throughout all eternity.

Following the Lord's ways and doing His will lead to great happiness and fulfillment. With God's help I will do so each day of my life. I realize that endurance leads to happiness, so I will persevere and endure no matter what I may face.

God has shown me that suffering for righteousness' sake will lead to happiness. Therefore, I will not be afraid of anyone or anything. Instead, I will sanctify the Lord God in my heart and be ready to give an answer to everyone who asks me a reason for the hope that I have in Christ.

I will not think it strange if I have to go through a fiery trial of any kind. Instead, I will rejoice, because I know I am a partaker of the sufferings of Christ. I know that when His glory is revealed, I will be glad with exceeding joy. If I am reproached for the name of Christ, I will be happy, for the Spirit of God and of glory rests upon me.

I am happy in the service of the King.

Scriptures: Job 5:17; Psalm 128:1-2; Psalm 144:15; Psalm 146; Proverbs 3:13; Proverbs3:18; Proverbs 14:21; John 13:17; James 5:11; 1 Peter 3:14; 1 Peter 4:14.

A Bible Prayer About Happiness: Father, thank

you for imparting your joy to me. It truly is my strength, my victory, and my happiness. I will ever rejoice because of all your blessings in my life and because I know you. I will shout for joy because I know you defend me. I truly am happy and blessed in your presence, Lord. Thank you for blessing me so richly. In Jesus' name, Amen.

A Word of Wisdom: *"Meditation keeps out Satan. It increases knowledge, it inflames love, it works, patience, it promotes prayer, and it evidences sincerity"* (Philip Henry). *It also increases your happiness!*

25

HEALING

❧

*If thou wilt diligently hearken to the voice
of the Lord thy God, and wilt do that
which is right in his sight, and wilt give ear
to his commandments, and keep all his
statutes, I will put none of these diseases
upon thee, which I have brought upon the
Egyptians: for I am the Lord that healeth thee.*
(Exodus 15:26)

Central Focus: Jesus is the Great Physician, and
the Lord is our Healer.

Points to Ponder: All healing comes from God,
the One who designed your body. He wants the
best for you. Jesus prayed, "Thy will be done in
earth, as it is in heaven" (Matthew 6:10). In Heaven
there is no sickness or disease. God's will is for
His children to walk in divine health. Remember,
nothing is too hard for Him.

Bible Meditation: Bless the Lord, O my soul: and
all that is within me, bless His holy name. Bless the
Lord, O my soul, and forget not all His benefits. He
forgives all my iniquities and heals all my diseases.
He redeems my life from destruction and crowns
me with loving-kindness and tender mercies. He
satisfies my mouth with good things so that my

youth is renewed like the eagle's.

The Lord heals the broken in heart, and He binds up my wounds. He is great and of great power. His understanding is infinite. He lifts up the meek. I will sing unto Him with thanksgiving and sing praise to Him. The Sun of righteousness is rising with healing in His wings.

Help me to always remember that Jesus is the Great Physician, and He is the same yesterday, today, and forever. He went about all Galilee, teaching in the synagogues and preaching the gospel of the Kingdom. He healed all manner of disease among the people, and His power is still available to us today.

I thank God that He anointed Jesus with the Holy Ghost and with power. He went about doing good and healing all that were oppressed by the devil, for God was with Him. This same Jesus lives within me and I can avail myself of His unlimited power at any time.

Gifts of healing come by way of the Holy Spirit, and the manifestation of the Holy Spirit has been given to each believer so that we would receive His blessings.

In times of sickness I will hope in God, for I shall yet praise Him who is the health of my countenance and my God. I will trust in Him with all my heart and not lean upon my own understanding. In all my ways I will acknowledge Him and I know He will direct my steps. I will not be wise in my own eyes. Instead, I will fear the Lord and depart from evil. This will bring good health to me.

I will attend to God's words at all times and incline my ear to His sayings. I will not let them depart from my eyes. I will keep them in the center of my heart, for they are life to me and health to my flesh. I will speak truth and show forth righteousness, realizing that the tongue of the wise is health. Yes, life and death are in the power of the tongue. I will remember that pleasant words are as a honeycomb, sweet to the soul, and health to the bones.

The promises of God's Word mean so much to me. He promises, "Then shall thy light break forth as the morning, and thine health shall spring forth speedily: and thy righteousness shall go before thee; the glory of the Lord shall be thy reward" (Isaiah 58:8). Praise the Lord for this wonderful promise.

Another promise from the Old Testament states: "For I will restore health unto thee, and I will heal thee of thy wounds, saith the Lord" (Jeremiah 30:17). Praise God!

Scriptures: Psalm 103:1–5; Psalm 147:1–7; Malachi 4:2; Hebrews 13:8; Matthew 4:23; Acts 10:38; 1 Corinthians 12:9; Psalm 42:11; Proverbs 3:5–8; Proverbs 4:20–22; Proverbs 12:17–18; Proverbs 18:21; Proverbs 16:24; Isaiah 58:8; Jeremiah 30:17.

A Bible Prayer About Healing: Father, I thank you for your Word which tells me to pray when I am afflicted and to call for the elders of the church so that they would pray over me and anoint me with oil in the name of the Lord. I will do this whenever I need healing, for I know that the prayer of faith will save the sick and the Lord will raise him up. Praise the Lord for these marvelous promises. In the name of the Great Physician I pray, Amen.

A Word of Wisdom: *"Meditation is the activity of calling to mind and thinking over, and dwelling on, and applying to oneself the various things that one knows about the works and ways and purpose and promises of God" (J.I. Packer).*

26
HOPE

Now the God of hope fill you with all joy and peace in believing, that ye may abound in hope, through the power of the Holy Ghost.
(Romans 15:13)

Central Focus: As believers, we are children of hope, because our Father is the God of all hope.

Points to Ponder: Hope is desire accompanied with expectation. This most certainly involves faith and trust. Hope is an expectation that one will get what one wants. Through hope we obtain both joy and peace. Hope is the anchor of our souls. Without hope it would be impossible to persevere, to believe, and to keep on keeping on.

Bible Meditation: Therefore being justified by faith, I have peace with God through the Lord Jesus Christ. Through Him I have access by faith into the grace wherein I stand and I rejoice in the hope of the glory of God. I glory in tribulations, because I know that tribulation works patience, patience works experience, and experience works hope. And it is hope that keeps me from ever being ashamed, because the love of God is shed abroad in my heart by the Holy Ghost which has been given to me.

With the Lord's help, I will let love be without hypocrisy in my life. I will abhor that which is evil and cleave to that which is good. I will be kindly affectioned toward others with brotherly love. In honor, I will prefer others over myself. I will not be slothful in business, but I will be fervent in spirit as I serve the Lord. I will rejoice in hope and be patient in tribulation, as I continue instant in prayer.

The God of hope is filling me with all joy and peace in believing, that I may abound in hope through the power of the Holy Spirit. The God of my Lord Jesus Christ, the Father of glory, is giving unto me the spirit of wisdom and revelation in the knowledge of Him. The eyes of my understanding are being enlightened, that I might know what the hope of His calling is and what the riches of His glory in His inheritance are. I thank God that He is showing me the exceeding greatness of His power to me.

According to my earnest expectation and my hope, I shall never be ashamed. With all boldness, as always, so now also Christ will be magnified in my body, whether it be by life or death. For to me to live is Christ, and to die is gain.

God is showing me the riches of the glory of the mystery which was hidden for ages, and this mystery is Christ in me, the hope of glory. Yes, Jesus lives within me and this gives me great hope. My hope, joy, and crown of rejoicing are related to the presence of Jesus Christ at His coming.

I am putting on the breastplate of faith and love, and my helmet is the hope of salvation. God loves me, and He has given me everlasting consolation and good hope through grace. The certainty of this knowledge comforts my heart and helps me to be established in every good word and work.

The Lord Jesus Christ truly is my hope. He gives me the hope of eternal life, which God, who cannot lie, promised before the world began. God's wonderful grace teaches me that I should deny ungodliness and worldly lusts. I should live soberly, righteously, and godly in the present world, as I look for the blessed hope, the glorious appearing of my great God and the Lord Jesus Christ, who gave himself for me, that He might redeem me from iniquity and purify me.

God is not unrighteous to forget my work and labor of love that I've done in His name. It is a great joy for me to minister to the saints. I will be diligent to show forth the full assurance of hope until the end. Hallelujah!

I lay hold on the hope that God has set before me. This hope is an anchor for my soul, both sure and steadfast. Blessed be the God and Father of my Lord Jesus Christ, who, according to His abundant mercy has begotten me unto a lively hope by the Resurrection of Jesus Christ from the dead. He has given me an incorruptible inheritance that is undefiled and that does not fade away. It is reserved in Heaven for me.

Scriptures: Romans 5:1-5; Romans 12:9-12; Romans 15:13; Ephesians 1:17-19; Philippians 1:20-21; Colossians 1:26-27; 1 Thessalonians 2:19; 1 Thessalonians 5:8; 2 Thessalonians 2:16-17; 1 Timothy 1:1; Titus 1:2; Titus 2:13-14; Hebrews 6:10; Hebrews 6:18; 1 Peter 1:3-4.

A Bible Prayer About Hope: Dear Lord, my heart is filled with hope because of all you have done for me. I look forward in hope to all you will do. Thank you, Lord. You are the God of all hope, and the fact that Christ lives within me gives me the hope of glory. The hope you've imparted to me keeps me from shame and fear. It leads me to trust you and to do good. Hope truly is the anchor of my soul. In Jesus' name I pray, Amen.

A Word of Wisdom: *"Holding the Word of God in your heart until it has affected every phase of your life—this is meditation"* (Andrew Murray).

27
HUMILITY

∞

*By humility and the fear of the Lord are riches,
and honour, and life.*
(Proverbs 22:4)

Central Focus: We must humble ourselves under God's almighty hand. In this way, we know He will exalt us in due time.

Points to Ponder: Humility is a quality of life that permits no pride, arrogance, or conceit. Humility conquers selfishness and self-centeredness, and it comes from submitting our lives to God. As we learn to humble ourselves under God's almighty hand, we will receive His grace and honor, and we will never need to promote ourselves in any way again.

Bible Meditation: As a body of believers, we must learn to humble ourselves, pray, and seek the face of Almighty God. When this happens, He will hear from Heaven, forgive our sins, and heal our land. What a wonderful promise this is!

God never forgets the cry of the humble. The Lord is King forever and ever. He hears the desire of the humble, and He prepares our hearts and causes our ears to hear. I will bless the Lord at all times.

His praise shall continually be in my mouth. My soul shall make its boast in the Lord, and the humble will hear me and be glad.

God is helping me to remember that pride goes before destruction and a haughty spirit before a fall. Therefore, I know it is better to be of a humble spirit with the lowly than to divide the spoil with the proud. While a man's pride will bring him low, honor shall uphold the humble in spirit.

The high and holy One who inhabits eternity dwells with him who is of a contrite and humble spirit. He revives the spirit of the humble and the hearts of the contrite ones. Hallelujah! I will humble myself as a child, because I know that child-like faith is needed for entrance into the Kingdom of Heaven.

God's Word promises that whosoever exalts himself shall be abased, but he that humbles himself shall be exalted. God keeps giving grace to me. He resists the proud, but He gives grace to the humble. Therefore, I submit myself to Him, and, as I resist the devil, he flees from me. I draw near to God, and He draws near to me. I cleanse my hands and I purify my heart. I humble myself in the sight of the Lord, and He is lifting me up.

I will serve the Lord with all humility of mind. I will

be clothed with humility, for I know that God resists the proud and gives grace to the humble. Therefore, I choose to humble myself under the mighty hand of God, that He may exalt me in due time. Hallelujah!

I cast all my cares upon Him, for I know He cares for me. I will be sober and vigilant, for I know that the enemy, as a roaring lion, walks about seeking whom he may devour. I will resist him steadfast in the faith, knowing that all my brethren are experiencing the same afflictions.

But the God of all grace, who has called me to His eternal glory by Christ Jesus, will complete, establish, strengthen, and settle me. To Him be glory and dominion forever and ever. I want the same mind that was in Christ Jesus, my Lord, to be in me. He made himself of no reputation and took upon Him the form of a servant. He was made in the likeness of humanity. Being found in fashion as a man, he humbled himself and became obedient unto death, even the death of the cross.

Therefore, God highly exalted Him and gave Him a name that is above every name, that at the name of Jesus every knee should bow and every tongue confess that Jesus Christ is Lord to the glory of God the Father.

Scriptures: 2 Chronicles 7:14; Psalm 9:12; Proverbs 10:16-17; Psalm 34:1-2; Proverbs 16:19; Proverbs 29:23; Isaiah 57:15; Matthew 18:3-4; Matthew 23:12; James 4:6-10; Acts 20:19; 1 Peter 5:5-10; Philippians 2:6-11.

A Bible Prayer About Humility: Abba-Father, I realize I have no reason whatsoever to feel proud, for all I am and have come from you. Without you I am nothing, but through you I can do all things. I humble myself, therefore, under your mighty hand with the certain knowledge that you will exalt me in due time. Thank you, Father. I love you, I adore you, and I submit my life to you. Use me in whatever ways you can. In Jesus' name I pray, Amen.

A Word of Wisdom: *"Meekness [humility] is not weakness! The one who is meek is the recipient of the power that comes from faith which is energized by God's Word. Not only is meekness a prerequisite for receiving the power of the Word, it is imperative in transmitting that Word to others"* (C. Paul Willis).

28
INTIMACY WITH GOD

❧

Draw nigh to God,
and he will draw nigh to you.
(James 4:8)

Central Focus: We were created to have fellowship with our heavenly Father. He loves us, and He wants intimacy with us.

Points to Ponder: The purpose for my creation was to have intimacy with God. This is what He wants, and it is what I want as well. As I draw near to Him, I know He draws near to me, and this knowledge helps me to understand that He will always be with me, never leave me, nor forsake me. His love has been shed abroad in my heart that I would be able to comprehend with all saints the full measure of His love and share it with others.

Bible Meditation: I want intimacy with God, my Father, who has adopted me into His family. I want to know Him as fully as possible. It is as I still myself in His presence that I am able to experience this wonderful intimacy with Him.

Intimacy with God is true fellowship with Him, and I want to have fellowship with Him and the

Lord Jesus Christ at all times. I will no longer walk in darkness. Instead, I will walk in the light, as He is in the light. This will greatly enhance my fellowship with Him and with other believers. The blood of Jesus Christ cleanses me from all sin—past, present, and future.

The grace of the Lord Jesus Christ, God's amazing love, and the communion of the Holy Ghost are mine to enjoy as I continue my relationship with the Lord. There is no relationship like this one. He is my Shepherd, and I want to live close to Him. He is so faithful to me, and I know I shall never suffer want. I will fear no evil, for I know He is always with me.

The promises of God's Word assure me that my intimacy with God will grow. His Word is a lamp unto my feet and a light unto my path. I will walk in the light of God's Word always. I know the Lord will never leave me nor forsake me.

God has reconciled me unto himself. He is helping me continue in the faith, grounded and settled, and I will not be moved away from the hope of the gospel. It is my very life. The Holy Spirit bears witness with my spirit that I am a child of God. Hallelujah!

God's everlasting love keeps me going. I will

always endeavor to be faithful to Him, as He is to me. I am so glad that He has searched me and known me. The truth is that He knows when I sit down and when I rise up. He even discerns my thoughts from afar.

He searches my path and my lying down, and He is acquainted with all my ways. Even before a word is on my tongue, He knows it altogether. I am so thankful that He hems me in, behind and before, and He lays His hand upon me.

He is my God, and I earnestly seek Him. My soul thirsts for Him. My flesh faints for him, as in a dry and weary land where there is no water. I have beheld His power and glory in the sanctuary. Because His loving-kindness is better than life to me, my lips shall praise Him and my soul shall be satisfied. With all my heart, soul, and might I will love Him for the rest of my days.

Scriptures: Psalm 46:10; 1 John 1:3; 1 John 1:4; 1 John 1:7; 2 Corinthians 13:14; Psalm 23:1; Psalm 23:4; Psalm 119:105; Hebrews 13:5; Colossians 1:21; Colossians 1:23; Romans 8:16; Jeremiah 31:3; Psalm 139:1–24; Psalm 6:1–11; Deuteronomy 6:5.

A Bible Prayer About Intimacy With God: Heavenly Father, in your wonderful presence there is fullness of joy and there are pleasures forever more. Thank you for creating me to have fellowship with you. I want to do my part to maintain that exciting relationship forever. Thank you for taking hold of my right hand. Thank you for allowing me to abide in Christ and to have fellowship with Him and with you. You are my portion, Lord God, and I will serve you forever. I will walk hand in hand with you. In Jesus' name I pray, Amen.

A Word of Wisdom: *"The habit of meditating on God's Word helps to induce the quiet heart and devout spirit which realizes the Lord's presence. The Bible is like the garden in which the Lord God walked in the cool of the day. Read it much and prayerfully and you will meet Him in its glades"* (F. B. Meyer).

29

LOVE

❧

The first of all the commandments is, Hear, O Israel; the Lord our God is one Lord: And thou shalt love the Lord thy God will all thy heart, and with all thy soul, and with all thy mind, and with all thy strength: this is the first commandment. And the second is like, namely this, Thou shalt love thy neighbour as thyself. There is none other commandment greater than these.
(Mark 12:29–31)

Central Focus: God loves you! His perfect love is everlasting. Respond to His love with faith, and realize that the only thing that counts is faith expressing itself through love.

Points to Ponder: Each person needs to love and be loved, and both of these needs are met in our relationship with the Lord. (See Romans 8:38–39.) He loves us with an everlasting love, and nothing shall ever be able to separate us from His love. We are able to love because He first loved us, and His perfect love casts all fear away from us. Through His mighty love we are able to be more than conquerors.

Bible Meditation: God is love. He wants me to

love others, for love is of God and everyone who loves is born of God and knows Him. He that does not love does not love God, for God is love. God sent His only Son into the world, that we would be able to live through Him.

Herein is love. Not that we loved God, but that He loved us and sent His Son to be a propitiation for our sins. For God so loved the world that He gave His only begotten Son, that whoever would believe on Him would not perish but would have eternal life. Hallelujah! This is incredible love.

God dwells in me and His love is perfected in me. I have known and believed the love that God has for me. He is love and I will dwell in love and so dwell in Him. Herein is my love made perfect, that I may have boldness in the day of judgment. As He is, so am I in this world.

I love Him because He first loved me. There is no fear in love, for His perfect love casts out all fear, because fear has torment, and I know that those who fear have not been made perfect in love. God's love has been shed abroad in my heart by the Holy Spirit who was given to me.

God commended His love toward me in that while I was yet a sinner Christ died for me. I know that all things work together for good in my life because I love God and He has called me according to His purpose. Who shall separate me from the love of Christ? Shall tribulation, distress, persecution, famine, nakedness, peril, or sword?

No, in all these things I am more than a conqueror through Christ who loves me. And I am persuaded that neither death, life, angels, principalities, powers, things present, things to come, height, depth, nor any other creature shall be able to separate me from the love of God, which is in Christ Jesus my Lord.

Love is the fulfilling of the Law. Through the Spirit I wait for the hope of righteousness by faith. The most essential thing is faith working by love, and I will walk in faith and love for the rest of my life.

The fruit of the Spirit is love, joy, peace, longsuffering, gentleness, goodness, faith, meekness, temperance, and against these things there is no law. I will always remember that God has not given me the spirit of fear but of love, power, and a sound mind. Hallelujah!

I realize that the trial of my faith is more precious than of gold that perishes, though it be tried by fire. May my faith be found unto praise and honor and glory at the appearing of the Lord

Jesus Christ. Even though I have never seen Him, I love Him. Believing in Him, I rejoice with joy unspeakable and full of glory, as I receive the end of my faith, the salvation of my soul.

Scriptures: 1 John 4:7-10; John 3:16; 1 John 4:12; 1 John 4:14-18; Romans 5:5; Romans 5:8; Romans 8:35-39; Romans 13:10; Galatians 5:6; Galatians 5:22-23; 1 Peter 1:7-9.

A Bible Prayer About Love: Thank you for shedding your love abroad in my heart, Father. Thank you for loving me so much that you adopted me into your family. I love you with all my heart, soul, and strength. I want my love toward others to be without hypocrisy at all times. I will love others and will never work ill toward anyone. With your help, Father, I will walk in love as Christ has loved me and has given himself as an offering and a sacrifice to you. Thank you, Father, for loving me and enabling me to love you and others. In Jesus' name, Amen.

A Word of Wisdom: *"If I ever try to secure a quiet half-hour's meditation upon His love to me, somebody is pretty sure to come and knock at the door. But if I can keep the door-knocker still, and get alone with my Lord and only think about His love to me—not trying to elaborate any theories, or to understand any doctrines,* *but just sitting down with the view of loving Him who gave himself for me—I tell you, Sirs, that this thought is positively inebriating to the soul"* (Charles H. Spurgeon).

30
PATIENCE

⚜

That ye be not slothful, but followers
of them who through faith and patience
inherit the promises.
(Hebrews 6:12)

Central Focus: The virtue of patience comes to us when we learn to wait upon the Lord.

Points to Ponder: Another word for patience is longsuffering, but actual patience, though sometimes challenging, never involves suffering, for true patience leads to hope, contentment, and trust. As we wait patiently in the Lord's presence many wonderful things happen, so let patience have its perfect work in your life, that you may be perfect and entire, wanting nothing. (See James 1:4.)

Bible Meditation: Through patience I am able to possess my own soul—the seat of my emotions, will, and intellect. In so doing I am able to remain focused on the Lord who is the source of perfect peace in my life.

I glory in tribulations in the knowledge that tribulation works patience into me. Through patience I gain experience and this experience gives me hope. Through hope I am never ashamed, because the love of God is shed abroad in my heart by the Holy Ghost who has been given to me.

I am saved by hope. I realize that hope that is seen is not really hope, for if something is in my presence I no longer need to hope for it. However, when I hope for what I do not see, patience teaches me to wait for it. Through the patience and comfort that the Word of God supplies to me I am able to cling to hope.

The God of patience and consolation is granting to me the ability to be like-minded with my fellow-believers according to Jesus Christ. Hallelujah!

My prayer is that I would walk worthy of the Lord unto all pleasing and be fruitful in every good work. May I increase in the knowledge of God and be strengthened with all might according to His glorious power, unto all patience with joyfulness.

I will give thanks to the Father who has made me meet to be a partaker of the inheritance of the saints in light. He has delivered me from the power of darkness and has translated me into the kingdom of His dear Son in whom I have redemption through His blood, even the forgiveness of sins.

With God's help I will be strong in the grace of

Jesus Christ. I will be sober, grave, temperate, and sound in faith, love, and patience. I never want to be slothful. Instead, through God's grace I will become a follower of all those who through faith and patience inherit the promises.

Seeing that I am compassed about by so great a cloud of witnesses, I will lay aside every weight and the sin that does so easily beset me and I will run with patience the race that is set before me, looking unto Jesus who is the author and finisher of my faith.

It was for the joy that was set before Him that Jesus endured the cross. Now He is sitting at the right hand of God's throne. This knowledge helps me to be peaceful and to understand the importance of patience in my own life.

The trying of my faith works patience into me, and I will let patience have her perfect work, that I may be perfect and entire, wanting nothing. I will be patient unto the coming of the Lord. I will establish my heart in God's ways and truth, for I know that the coming of the Lord is drawing near. Hallelujah!

I am so thankful for all the great and precious promises of God that I find in His Word. By these I am enabled to be a partaker of His divine nature, having escaped the corruption that is in the world through lust. I will give all diligence to add virtue to my faith, knowledge to my virtue, temperance to my knowledge, patience to my temperance, godliness to my temperance, brotherly kindness to my godliness, and love to my brotherly kindness.

I will trust in the Lord and do good. I will delight myself in the Lord, and I know He will give me the desires of my heart. I will commit my way unto the Lord and trust also in Him, and I know He will bring it to pass. Indeed, He shall bring forth my righteousness as the light. Therefore, I will rest in Him and wait patiently for Him.

Scriptures: Luke 21:19; Isaiah 26:3; Romans 5:3-5; Romans 8:24-25; Romans 15:4-5; Colossians 1:10-14; 2 Timothy 2:1; Titus 2:2; Hebrews 6:11-12; James 1:3-4; James 5:7-8; 2 Peter 1:4-7; Psalm 37:3-7.

A Bible Prayer About Patience: Thank you, Father, for your love in my life which leads me into patience. Your love is patient and kind. I wait patiently for you, Lord. As I wait and hope for what I do not have, I do so patiently, because I know you will supply all my need according to your riches in glory by Christ Jesus. Help me always to be patient in hope, affliction, and prayer. In the name of Jesus I pray, Amen.

A Word of Wisdom: *"There's no music in a 'rest,' . . . but there's the making of music in it. And people are always missing that part of the life melody, . . . always talking of perseverance and courage and fortitude; but patience is the finest and worthiest part of fortitude, and the rarest, too"* (Ruskin).

31

PEACE

❧

Thou wilt keep him in perfect peace,
whose mind is stayed on thee:
because he trusteth in thee.
(Isaiah 26:3)

Central Focus: God's peace is like a river that flows through our hearts. His peace helps us to remain calm in all circumstances.

Points to Ponder: God wants you to experience His perfect peace, which surpasses all understanding. He does not want your heart to worry or be afraid. Jesus said, "Peace I leave with you, my peace I give unto you: not as the world giveth, give I unto you. Let not your heart be troubled, neither let it be afraid" (John 14:27). Perfect peace is available to you. Take it and let it soak into your innermost being.

Bible Meditation: I will be anxious about nothing, but in every situation by prayer and supplication with thanksgiving I will let my request be made known unto God. As I do so, I know that His marvelous peace, which surpasses all understanding, will keep my heart and mind through Christ Jesus. This is true peace.

The God of peace is always with me. It pleased the Father that all fullness should dwell in Jesus, and, having made peace through the blood of His cross, by Him to reconcile all things unto himself. I am so thankful that I've been reconciled to God, and this gives me great peace.

I will let the peace of God rule in my heart, and I will be thankful. I will let the Word of Christ dwell in me richly in all wisdom, and whatever I do in word or deed, I will do all in the name of the Lord Jesus, giving thanks to God and the Father by Him.

I will rejoice evermore, pray without ceasing, and give thanks in everything, for I know this is the will of God in Christ Jesus concerning me. I will never quench the Spirit. I will prove all things and hold fast to that which is good. I will abstain from every appearance of evil. As a result, I know that the peace of God will sanctify me wholly and my whole spirit, soul, and body will be preserved blameless unto the coming of the Lord Jesus Christ.

As I lift up my hands and make straight paths for my feet, I will follow peace with all others. I will follow holiness, as well, without which no one will see the Lord. I will look diligently lest anyone fail of the grace of God and lest any root of bitterness spring up to trouble me and many be defiled.

The God of peace that brought again from the dead our Lord Jesus, that great shepherd of the sheep, through the blood of the everlasting covenant, is making me perfect in every good work to do His will. He is working into me that which is pleasing in His sight. Unto Him be glory forever and ever.

I will keep my tongue from evil and my lips from speaking guile. I will depart from evil and go good, and I will seek and pursue peace. I thank God for the promise that the meek will inherit the Earth and shall delight themselves in the abundance of peace. I take my delight in such abundance.

I have great peace because I love God's law, and I know that nothing shall offend me. I will never forget God's law, and I will always endeavor to keep His commandments. The result in my life will be long life and peace. Hallelujah!

God has given me His wisdom and spiritual understanding, and this makes me happy. Wisdom is more precious to me than rubies and there is nothing I can desire that will compare with it. Length of days, riches, and honor are to be found in God's wisdom.

All the paths of wisdom are peace and all the

paths of wisdom are pleasant. God keeps me in perfect peace as my mind is stayed on Him. I trust Him forever, for I know that the Lord Jehovah is everlasting strength for me.

I will trust in Him with all my heart, without leaning upon my own understanding. In all my ways I will acknowledge Him and I know He will direct my steps. I love God's Word. It will never return unto Him void, but shall accomplish that which He pleases and it shall prosper in the thing whereto He sends it. This is such a wonderful promise.

It makes me know that I shall always be able to go out with joy and be led forth with peace. I thank God that the Dayspring from on High has visited me. He has given light to me, and He guides my feet in the pathway of peace.

Scriptures: Philippians 4:6-7; Philippians 4:9; Colossians 1:19-20; Colossians 3:13-17; 1 Thessalonians 5:16-23; Hebrews 12:12-15; Hebrews 13:20-21; Psalm 34:13-14; Psalm 37:11; Psalm 119:165; Proverbs 3:1-2; Proverbs 3:13-17; Proverbs 26:3-4; Proverbs 3:5-6; Isaiah 55:11-12; Luke 1:79.

A Bible Prayer About Peace: Great God of peace, thank you for blessing me with a supernatural peace that guards my heart and my mind. I realize that I have no need to be anxious about anything, but through prayer and supplication with thanksgiving, I will let my requests be made known to you. When I do this, your wonderful peace that surpasses all understanding fills me with certainty and protection. Thank you, for your peace, Father.

A Word of Wisdom: *"We are conformed to Him in proportion as our lives grow in quietness, His peace spreading within our souls. Even amid all that outwardly disturbs us we have, if we have Him, the same peace, because He is our peace, sustaining our whole being"* (T.T. Carter).

32

POWER

❦

*Finally, my brethren, be strong in the Lord,
and in the power of his might.*
(Ephesians 6:10)

Central Focus: God's power is at work in your life. Let it come forth, and you will be a victorious Christian.

Points to Ponder: The Holy Spirit is the source of power in my life. He dwells within me, and His power is available to me all the time. His power enables me to witness effectively and to be victorious over all enemies. God's power is greater than any power known to mankind, for it is able to release miracles and help us with all our problems.

Bible Meditation: The God of my Lord Jesus Christ, the Father of glory, is giving me the spirit of wisdom and revelation in the knowledge of Him. The eyes of my understanding are being enlightened, that I might know the hope of His calling and what the riches of the glory of His inheritance are. Moreover, He is helping to experience the exceeding greatness of His power as I believe, according to the working of His mighty power which He wrought in Christ when

He raised Him from the dead and set Him at His own right hand in the heavenly places, far above all principality, power, might, dominion, and every name that is named, not only in this world, but also in that which is to come. Hallelujah!

He is able to do exceeding abundantly above all that I ask or think, according to the power that works within me. Unto Him be glory in the Church by Christ Jesus throughout all ages, world without end.

I count all things but loss for the excellency of the knowledge of Christ Jesus my Lord: for whom I have suffered the loss of all things and do count them but dung, that I may win Christ and be found in Him, not having my own righteousness, which is of the law, but that which is through the faith of Christ, the righteousness which is of God by faith, that I may know Him and the power of His resurrection as well as the fellowship of His sufferings, being made conformable to His death.

It is my heart's desire to walk worthy of the Lord unto all pleasing and to be fruitful in every good work, as I increase in the knowledge of God. He is strengthening me with all might, according to His glorious power, unto all patience and longsuffering with joyfulness. I give thanks unto the Father for His mighty power.

The gospel has come to me not in word only, but also in power and in the Holy Ghost and in much assurance. I thank God that He has counted me worthy of His calling. He is fulfilling all the good pleasure of His goodness and the work of faith with power, that the name of the Lord Jesus Christ would be glorified in me, according to the grace of God and the Lord Jesus Christ.

God has not given me the spirit of fear, but of power, love, and a sound mind. Hallelujah! Therefore, I am not ashamed of the testimony of my Lord, nor of me His prisoner. I thank God that I have been allowed to be a partaker of the afflictions of the gospel according to the power of God who has saved me and called me with a holy calling, not according to my own works, but according to His purpose and grace, which were given to me in Christ Jesus.

Blessed be the God and Father of my Lord Jesus Christ, who according to His abundant mercy has begotten me unto a lively hope by the resurrection of Jesus Christ from the dead to an incorruptible and undefiled inheritance that never fades away and is reserved in Heaven for me. I am being kept by the power of God through faith unto salvation that will be revealed to me in the last time.

Therefore, I greatly rejoice, for I know that the

trial of my faith, being much more precious than of gold that perishes, though it be tried by fire, might be found unto praise and honor and glory at the appearing of Jesus Christ, who having not seen, I love. In Him, though now I do not see Him, yet believing, I rejoice with joy unspeakable and full of glory, receiving the end of my faith, even the salvation of my soul.

Grace and peace are being multiplied to me through the knowledge of God and of Jesus, my Lord. According as His divine power has given unto me all things that pertain to life and godliness through the knowledge of Him who has called me to glory and virtue. He has given me exceedingly great and precious promises, that by these I would become a partaker of His divine nature, having escaped the corruption that is in the world through lust.

Now unto Him who is able to keep me from falling and to present me faultless before the presence of His glory with exceeding joy. To the only wise God, my Savior, be glory, majesty, dominion, and power both now and evermore. Amen.

Scriptures: Ephesians 1:17-21; Ephesians 3:20-21; Philippians 3:8-10; Colossians 1:10-12; 1 Thessalonians 1:5; 2 Thessalonians 1:11-12; 2 Timothy 1:7; 2 Timothy 1:8-9; 1 Peter 1:3-9;

2 Peter 1:2–4; Jude 24–25.

A Bible Prayer About Power: Father–God, your power is made perfect in my weakness. Thank you for your great power with which nothing can compare. Let your power rest upon me and fill me. You give strength to the weary and you increase the power of the weak. Thank you for your promise which assures me that you are able to do exceeding abundantly above all that I ask or think, according to your power which is at work within me. I will let your power flow through me. Thank you, my powerful Lord.

A Word of Wisdom: *"When we cultivate the inner person through prayer, meditation on the Word, and submission to the Lord, then we can experience the joys of a disciplined and diligent life"* (Warren Wiersbe).

33
PROTECTION

❦

For he shall give his angels charge over thee,
to keep thee in all thy ways.
(Psalm 91:11)

Central Focus: God is your defender, your deliverer, and your place of refuge.

Points to Ponder: God is your Father, and He loves you with an everlasting love. He will take good care of you and protect you. He is your fortress, your high tower, and your defense from all attacks. He fights for you. He is with you and He will never leave you nor forsake you. All you have to do is place all your trust in Him, "casting all your care upon him; for he careth for you" (1 Peter 5:7).

Bible Meditation: I am dwelling in the secret place of the Most High, and I am abiding under the shadow of the Almighty. I will say of the Lord that He is my refuge and my fortress. He is my God, and in Him will I trust. I know He will deliver me from the snare of the fowler and from the noisome pestilence. His protection protects me in every situation. Hallelujah!

He is covering me with his feathers, and under His wings I shall forever trust. His truth is my shield and buckler. Because I know these things are true, I will not be afraid of any terror at night nor of any arrows that fly during the day. I will not fear any pestilence or disease. A thousand may fall at my side and 10,000 at my right hand, but I know I will be protected.

Because I have made the Lord, who is my refuge, my habitation, I know that no evil will befall me, and no plague will come near my dwelling. He is giving His angels charge over me, to keep me in all my ways. They will bear me up in their hands, lest I should dash my foot against a stone. As I call upon His name, I know He will answer me. He will be with me in times of trouble. He will deliver me and honor me. Praise the Lord!

The Lord is my light and my salvation. Whom shall I fear? The Lord is the strength of my life. Of what shall I be afraid? In the time of trouble, He will hide me in His pavilion. In the secret place of His pavilion He will hide me. He will set me upon a rock. My head shall be lifted up above my enemies round about me.

I will love the Lord, for He is my strength. He is my rock and my fortress. He is my deliverer, my God, and my strength. I will trust in Him. He is my buckler and the horn of my salvation. He is my high tower. I will call upon Him, for He is worthy to be praised, and so shall I be saved from my enemies.

With God's help I am able to run through a troop and leap over a wall. As for God, His way is perfect. His Word is tried, and He is a buckler to all that trust in Him. I trust in Him with all my heart. My defense is of God. I wait upon God, for He is my defense. He will protect me from all enemies.

No weapon that is formed against me shall prosper, and every tongue that shall rise against me in judgment the Lord will condemn, for this is my heritage as His servant. Praise you, Lord. I put all my trust in Him, and I know I shall be safe.

I will be strong in the Lord and in the power of His might, as I put on His protective armor, which will enable me to stand against all the wiles of the devil. I realize that I do not wrestle against flesh and blood, but against principalities, powers, the rulers of the darkness of this world, and spiritual wickedness in high places.

God's armor enables me to withstand in the evil day, and, having done all, to stand. I take my stand upon God's Word, His promises, His truth, and His righteousness, and I know I shall prevail. I will ever remember that the Lord is my defense. My God is the rock of my refuge.

The angel of the Lord encamps around me. God is my refuge and my strength, a very present help in time of trouble. Therefore, I will not fear, no matter what happens. There is a river and its streams make me glad. God is in our midst. Therefore, I shall not be moved. I know God will help me. The Lord of hosts is with me. Hallelujah!

Scriptures: Psalm 91; Psalm 27:1; Psalm 27:5-6; Psalm 18:1-3; Psalm 18:32-33; Psalm 7:10; Psalm 59:9; Psalm 89:18; Isaiah 54:17; Proverbs 29:25; Ephesians 6:10-13; Ephesians 6:14; Psalm 34:7; Psalm 46.

A Bible Prayer About Protection: Dear Father, I know you are protecting me and that you love to take care of me. Thank you so much. You are mighty and awesome, and I will trust in you, for you are my shield and the horn of my salvation. You are my high tower, my refuge, and my Savior. I feel totally secure in you. Thank you for saving me from all violence and harm and for giving your angels charge over me. In Jesus' name I pray, Amen.

A Word of Wisdom: *"In the inner stillness where meditation leads, the Spirit secretly anoints the soul and heals our deepest wounds"* (St. John of the Cross).

34

REPENTANCE

≋

The goodness of God leadeth thee
to repentance.
(Romans 2:4)

Central Focus: To repent means that you will no longer live according to your own desires, but that you will desire to follow in the footsteps of your Lord. Decide to follow Jesus every step of your way.

Points to Ponder: Repentance involves turning away from sin and turning to God. Godly sorrow works repentance into our hearts. We must learn to confess our sins in the realization that God will forgive us our sins and cleanse us from all unrighteousness. (See 1 John 1:9.) It is the precious blood of Jesus that cleanses us of all sin—past, present, and future.

Bible Meditation: I repent of all my sins, because I know the Kingdom of God is at hand. With God's help I will bring forth fruit that is worthy of repentance. It is so wonderful to know the extent of joy in Heaven over one sinner who repents.

I thank God for His goodness which leads me

to repentance when I sin. Godly sorrow works repentance into me, and I am so grateful for this, because I know that worldly sorrow leads to death. As a result of repentance, I will flee youthful lusts, follow righteousness, faith, charity, and peace with all who call on the Lord out of a pure heart.

I will avoid foolish and unlearned questions, because they generate strife. As the Lord's servant, I know I shall not strive. It is important for me to be gentle unto all, apt to teach, and patient. This is my desire. In meekness I will instruct those that oppose themselves in the hope that God will give them repentance to the acknowledging of the truth and that they would be able to recover themselves out of the snare of the devil who has taken them captive.

One day is with the Lord as a thousand years and a thousand years as one day. I thank God for all the promises of His Word and for the fact that He is never slack concerning His promises. He is so patient toward me. It thrills me to know that He is not willing for anyone to perish, but that all should come to repentance. It is my desire to be used by Him to bring others to repentance, because the day of the Lord will come as a thief in the night.

Blessed be the God and Father of my Lord Jesus

Christ who has blessed me with all spiritual blessings in heavenly places in Christ. I thank Him that He chose me to be holy and blameless before Him in love. He has predestinated me to be His adopted child by Christ Jesus, according to the good pleasure of His will, to the praise of the glory of His grace, wherein He accepted me in the beloved.

In Christ I have redemption through His blood, the forgiveness of sins, according to the riches of His grace wherein He has abounded toward me in all wisdom and prudence. I am so thankful that He has made known unto me the mystery of His will, according to His good pleasure which He has purposed in himself. Hallelujah!

Through Christ I have obtained an inheritance, being predestinated according to the purpose of Him who works all things after the counsel of His own will, that we should be to the praise of His glory. I trust in Christ and I have been sealed with the Holy Spirit of promise, which is the earnest of my inheritance until the redemption of the purchased possession, unto the praise of His glory.

God, the Father of glory, is giving unto me the spirit of wisdom and revelation in the knowledge of Him. The eyes of my understanding are being enlightened, that I might know what is the hope of His calling and what the riches of the glory of His inheritance are. He is revealing to me the exceeding greatness of His power to me as I believe, according to the working of His mighty power.

All of these blessings—this marvelous inheritance—have come to me as a result of repentance.

Scriptures: Matthew 3:2; Luke 3:8; Luke 15:7; Romans 2:4; 2 Corinthians 7:10; 2 Timothy 2:22-26; 2 Peter 3:8-10; Ephesians 1:3-18.

A Bible Prayer About Repentance: Heavenly Father, I thank you for leading me into repentance. Your goodness and mercy to me are so wonderful. I thank you that you have buried my sins in the depths of the deepest sea, never to remember them ever again. I thank you that you have removed my sins from me as far as the east is from the west. The blood of Jesus Christ cleanses me from all sin. Hallelujah! In Jesus' name I pray, Amen.

A Word of Wisdom: *"Every time God forgives us, God is saying that God's own rules do not matter as much as the relationship that God wants to create with us"* (Richard Rohr).

35
REST

❧

*Come unto me, all ye that labour and are
heavy laden, and I will give you rest.*
*Take my yoke upon you, and learn of me;
for I am meek and lowly in heart: and*
*ye shall find rest unto your souls. For my yoke
is easy and my burden is light.*
(Matthew 11:28–30)

Central Focus: Resting in God means you will no longer have to strive. You will experience His peace, and His peace will guard your heart and your mind.

Points to Ponder: In the same way that God rested on the seventh day after creation, He has provided spiritual rest for us, and He wants us to learn to rest in Him. Several things, however, will prevent us from entering His rest, and some of these are: disobedience, unbelief, and hardness of heart. Jesus invites us to come and He will give us rest. Be yoked with Him, for His yoke is easy and His burden is light.

Bible Meditation: There remains a rest for the people of God. I will cease from striving and laboring in my own efforts, and I will enter into His rest, for I know that the Word of God is powerful and sharper than any two-edged sword. It is able to pierce even to the dividing asunder of soul and spirit, and of the joints and marrow, and it is a discerner of the thoughts and intents of the heart.

I will rest in the Lord and wait patiently for Him. I will trust in Him and do good. I will delight myself in Him, and I know He will give me the desires of my heart. I will commit my way unto the Lord and trust in Him, and He shall bring it to pass.

My flesh will rest in hope. To be spiritually minded is life and peace. The Kingdom of God is not meat and drink, but righteousness, peace, and joy through the Holy Ghost. God will keep me in perfect peace and rest if I keep my mind stayed on Him, because I trust Him.

The Lord is my shepherd. I shall not want. He makes me to lie down in green pastures. He leads me beside the still waters. He restores my soul. Hallelujah! God has given me His peace. Therefore, I will not let my heart be troubled or afraid.

I will be anxious about nothing, but in everything through prayer and supplication with thanksgiving I will let my requests be made known unto God, and His supernatural peace, which surpasses all understanding shall guard my mind and my heart through Christ Jesus.

The God of peace who brought Jesus Christ from the dead, that great shepherd of the sheep, through the blood of the everlasting covenant is making me perfect in every good work to do His will, and He is working in me that which is well-pleasing in His sight (including being able to rest), through Jesus Christ, to whom be glory and honor forever and ever.

I will let the Word of Christ dwell in me richly in all wisdom, and I will teach and admonish others in psalms, hymns, and spiritual songs, singing with grace in my heart to the Lord. Whatever I do in word of deed I will do in the name of the Lord Jesus, giving thanks to God and the Father through Him. I will let the peace of Christ and His rest rule in my heart, and I will be thankful.

I will rest in the Lord.

Scriptures: Hebrews 4:9-12; Psalm 37:3-7; Acts 2:26; Romans 8:2; Romans 14:17; Isaiah 26:3; Psalm 23:1-3; Philippians 4:6-7; Hebrews 13:20-21; Colossians 3:15-17.

A Bible Prayer About Rest: Heavenly Father, thank you so much for providing rest for me. I enter it with joy, and I leave behind all my burdens. Thank you for your promise of rest, which I now claim for my own life. I will cease from my own striving and let your rest flow through me. As I learn to take my rest in you, I will cease from my own striving. I will walk away from all unbelief, hardness of heart, and disobedience, for I know that these things will prevent me from entering your rest. In Jesus' name I pray, Amen.

A Word of Wisdom: *"There is such a thing as sacred idleness"* (George MacDonald).

36

RIGHTEOUSNESS

❧

*Lead me, O Lord, in thy righteousness
because of mine enemies; make thy way
straight before my face.*
(Psalm 5:8)

Central Focus: When we surrender everything to the Lord, we are filled with His righteousness and all self-righteousness is behind us.

Points to Ponder: In and of ourselves we have no righteousness. All of our righteousness is as filthy rags in God's sight. Jesus became sin for us so that we might become righteous through Him. He is our righteousness. When we confess our sins to Him, He forgives us and cleanses us from all unrighteousness. Let us determine to walk in righteousness every day of our lives.

Bible Meditation: Who shall abide in the Lord's tabernacle? Who shall dwell in His holy hill? These places are available to all who walk uprightly, work righteousness, and speak truth. It is my desire to be such a person before the Lord.

The Lord is leading me in His righteousness. He is making His way straight before me. Hallelujah! The Lord, my Shepherd, is leading me in the paths of righteousness for His name's sake. As I commit my way unto the Lord and wait patiently for Him, He will bring forth my righteousness as the light.

My mouth shall show forth the Lord's righteousness and His salvation all the day. I will go forth in the strength of the Lord God. I will mention His righteousness wherever I go. God's Word is very pure, and I love it. His righteousness is everlasting, and His law is the truth. The righteousness of His testimonies is everlasting. He is giving me understanding, and I shall live.

I will let others know about God's goodness and righteousness, and I will speak of His graciousness. He is full of compassion and of great mercy. He is slow to anger, and He is good to all. His tender mercies are over all His works.

Treasures of wickedness profit nothing, but righteousness delivers from death. The Lord will not permit the soul of the righteous to perish. In the way of righteousness is life; and in the pathway thereof there is no death. Praise the Lord!

Righteousness keeps me as long as I walk uprightly, but wickedness overthrows the sinner. Knowing that the Lord loves those who follow after righteousness, I will walk in His righteousness each step of my way. I want to remember that better is a little with righteousness than great revenues without it.

I will follow after righteousness and mercy, and so shall I find life, righteousness, and honor. The Lord Jesus Christ is made unto me wisdom, righteousness, sanctification, and redemption. I am being renewed in the spirit of my mind, as I put on the new man which, after God, is created in righteousness and true holiness.

I pray that my love may abound yet more and more, that I may be sincere and without offense till the day of Christ. I will be filled with the fruits of righteousness, which are by Jesus Christ unto the praise and glory of God.

I count all things but loss for the excellency of the knowledge of Christ Jesus my Lord for whom I have suffered the loss of all things, and do count them but dung, that I may win Christ. I always want to be found in Him, not having my own righteousness, which is of the law, but that which is through the faith of Christ, the righteousness which is of God by faith. That I may know Him and the power of His resurrection and the fellowship of His sufferings, being made conformable to His death, if by any means I might attain unto the resurrection of the dead.

I will follow after righteousness, godliness, faith, love, patience, and meekness. I will fight the good fight of faith and lay hold onto eternal life to which I have been called.

Scriptures: Psalm 15:1-2; Psalm 5:8; Psalm 23:3; Psalm 37:6; Psalm 71:15-16; Psalm 119:142-144; Psalm 145:7-11; Proverbs 10:2-3; Proverbs 12:28; Proverbs 13:6; Proverbs 15:9; Proverbs 16:8; Proverbs 21:21; 1 Corinthians 1:30; Ephesians 4:23-24; Philippians 1:9-11; Philippians 3:8-11; 1 Timothy 6:11-12.

A Bible Prayer About Righteousness: Dear Father, thank you for giving me your righteousness. It amazes me to know that Jesus became sin for me that I might become your righteousness through Him. May I always follow after righteousness, compassion, mercy, and grace. Thank you for cleansing me from all unrighteousness through the blood of Jesus Christ. In His name I pray, Amen.

A Word of Wisdom: *"Meditation is the grand means of our growth in grace; without it, prayer itself is an empty service"* (Charles Simeon).

37

SAFETY AND SECURITY

❦

Thou hast put gladness in my heart, more than in the time that their corn and their wine increased. I will both lay me down in peace, and sleep: for thou, Lord, only makest me dwell in safety.
(Psalm 4:7–8)

Central Focus: We are safe and secure when we allow God to be our abode. Dwell in Him, and you will not fear anything at all.

Points to Ponder: To feel safe and secure is vitally important in the day in which we live. In times like these we need to know that Jesus is protecting us in each and every circumstance we face. God's Word assures us that His protection is available to us, so that we will dwell in safety and security. He gives His angels charge over us, and He delivers us from all evil. His perfect love casts out all fear from our lives.

Bible Meditation: God is upholding me according to His Word, that I may live. He will never let me be ashamed of my hope. As He holds me up, I know I shall be safe. I will have respect unto His statutes at all times.

The name of the Lord is a strong tower. As I run into it, I know I shall be safe. I put all my trust in the Lord, and I know I shall be safe. I will follow the Lord's will and His statutes. I will keep His judgments and do them. In so doing, I know I will dwell in the land in safety. Praise His holy name.

It thrills me to know that I am one of the Lord's beloved and that I shall dwell in safety because He loves me. God has put gladness in my heart more than in the time that their corn and wine increased. Therefore, I will lie down in peace and sleep, for the Lord makes me dwell in safety.

Where no counsel is, the people fail, but I will remember that in the multitude of counselors there is safety. I will also remember that the horse is prepared against the day of battle, but safety is of the Lord. The Lord is my rock, and my fortress, and my deliverer. I will trust in Him. He is my shield, the horn of my salvation, my high tower, my refuge, and my Savior. He saves me from all violence. Hallelujah!

I will call on the Lord, who is worthy to be praised. So shall I be saved from my enemies. Blessed be the Lord my strength. He teaches my hands to war and my fingers to fight. He is my goodness, my deliverer, my shield, and the One in whom I trust. He subdues enemies under me.

The Lord is my strength, my fortress, and my refuge in the day of affliction. The Lord is my refuge and my strength. He is my very present help in trouble. Therefore, I will not fear, for I know I am safe in Him. God is my rock and my salvation. He is my sure defense. I shall not be moved. My soul, wait only upon God, for my expectation is from Him.

He only is my rock and my salvation. He is my defense. In God is my salvation and my glory. He is the rock of my strength and my refuge. He is my safe place. I will trust Him at all times and pour my heart out before Him.

My God is a strength unto the poor, a strength to the needy in his distress, a refuge from the storm, and a shadow from the heat. He keeps me safe and secure at all times. He will swallow up death in victory and will wipe away all tears, for the Lord has spoken this and promised this to me.

In my God I have found strong consolation. I have fled to Him for refuge and I have laid hold of the hope He has set before me. The hope He gives is an anchor for my soul that is both sure and steadfast. As I trust in the Lord and do good, I know He will take care of me. As I delight myself in Him, I know He will give me the desires of my heart.

The Lord is my shepherd. I shall not want. He makes me to lie down in green pastures. He leads me beside the still waters. He restores my soul and leads me in the path of righteousness for His name's sake. Yea, though I walk through the valley of the shadow of death, I will fear no evil, for I know He is with me. His rod and His staff comfort me. Surely goodness and mercy shall follow me all the days of my life, and I will dwell in the house of the Lord forever. Hallelujah!

Scriptures: Psalm 119:116–117; Proverbs 18:10; Proverbs 29:25; Leviticus 25:18; Deuteronomy 33:12; Psalm 4:7–8; Proverbs 11:14; Proverbs 21:31; 2 Samuel 22:1–4; Psalm 144:1–2; Jeremiah 16:19; Psalm 46:1–2; Psalm 62:1–7; Isaiah 25:4; Isaiah 25:8; Hebrews 6:18–19; Psalm 37:3–4; Psalm 23.

A Bible Prayer About Safety and Security: Father, thank you for allowing me to hide in you. My life is hidden in you through Christ. You are my safe place, and you are my total strength and security. You are my light and salvation, and I will not fear what anyone or anything can do to me. I am yours and you are mine. I reach out and take hold of your hand. Underneath me are your everlasting arms. I love you, Lord, and I place all my trust in you. In Jesus' name I pray, Amen.

A Word of Wisdom: *"The vessels are fullest of*

grace which are nearest its spring. The more Christ's glory is beheld, the more men are changed" (William Bagshawe).

38
SELF-CONTROL

❧

But the fruit of the Spirit is love, joy, peace,
longsuffering, gentleness, goodness,
faith, meekness, temperance [self-control]:
against such there is no law.
(Galatians 5:22-23)

Central Focus: Self-control is virtually impossible unless we are under the Master's control. His Spirit dwelling within you enables you to practice moderation and temperance in all that you do.

Points to Ponder: When we allow Jesus to be the Lord of our lives, we come under His control, and this is the source of self-control in our lives. We must let the Holy Spirit who lives within us take complete control of our lives, then we will bear His fruit in all our relationships and responsibilities. He helps us to keep our lives well-balanced and fruitful.

Bible Meditation: As I strive for the mastery of my life, I know I must be temperate and moderate in all things. With God's help I will keep my body, soul, and spirit under subjection.

Through God's grace I will endeavor to be blameless, as the steward of God. I will not be self-willed, given to anger or to wine, and I will not be given to money. Instead, I want to be hospitable to all, a loving follower of Christ, sober, just, holy, and temperate.

I will hold fast the faithful Word that I've been taught, that I may be able to be a good witness to others. I will rejoice in the Lord always and let my moderation be known unto all, for the Lord is at hand. I will be anxious about nothing, but in everything by prayer and supplication with thanksgiving I will let my requests be made known unto God. As I do so, I know that His supernatural peace that surpasses all understanding shall guard my heart and my mind through Christ Jesus.

I will think on whatsoever things that are true, honorable, just, pure, lovely, and of good report. If there be any virtue and if there be any praise, I will think on these things. I will do the things I've seen and heard from God's Word, and I know the God of peace will be with me.

I rejoice in the Lord greatly. Not that I speak in respect of want, for I have learned in whatsoever state I am, therewith to be content. I know both how to be abased and I know how to abound. Everywhere and in all things I am instructed both to be full and to be hungry, both to abound and to suffer need.

I can do all things through Christ who strengthens me, but without Him I can do nothing. The law of the Spirit of life in Christ Jesus has set me free from the law of sin and death, and now I realize that to be carnally minded is death, but to be spiritually minded is life and peace.

Because Christ lives within me, my body is dead because of sin, but the spirit is life because of righteousness. The Spirit of Him who raised Jesus from the dead lives in me and He is quickening my mortal body. Therefore, I know I am a debtor not to the flesh, to live after the flesh. Through the Holy Spirit I will mortify the deeds of my body, and thereby I shall live.

I will be led by God's Spirit, as one of His precious children. Hallelujah! I am so thankful that I have not received the spirit of bondage which leads to fear, but I have received the spirit of adoption whereby I am able to cry, "Abba, Father."

The Holy Spirit helps me in my infirmities, for I do not know what I should pray for as I ought. He makes intercession for us with groanings that cannot be uttered. I am thankful for God's promise which says that all things work together for good to those who love God and are called according to His purpose. Hallelujah!

When I lack wisdom, I will ask for it from God. I know He will give it to me when I ask in faith, nothing wavering. I will be single-minded in my purpose, my devotion, my goals, and my spiritual walk, for I know that a double-minded person is unstable in all his ways.

It makes me happy to be able to endure temptation, for I know that when I am tried I shall receive the crown of life, which the Lord has promised to those who love Him. I thank Him that every good and perfect gift comes from Him, the Father of lights, with whom there is no variableness nor shadow of turning. Therefore, I will be swift to hear, slow to speak, and slow to wrath.

With God's help I will walk in temperance, meekness, moderation, and self-control.

Scriptures: 1 Corinthians 9:25-27; Philippians 4:13; Titus 1:7-8; Titus 1:9; Philippians 4:4-14; John 15:5; Romans 8; James 1:5-19.

A Bible Prayer About Self-Control: Father-God, I know you are the blessed controller of all things in my life. I yield to your control, to your Lordship in every area of my life. I submit my life to you, and I commit myself to following your ways in all things. I will practice self-control through the power of your Holy Spirit who lives within me. Thank you for His power in my life. In Jesus' name, Amen.

A Word of Wisdom: *"I choose self-control. . . . I am a spiritual being. After this body is dead, my spirit will soar. I refuse to let what will rot, rule the eternal. I choose self-control. I will be drunk only by joy. I will be impassioned only by my faith. I will be influenced only by God. I will be taught only by Christ. I choose self-control"* (Max Lucado).

39

SOUNDNESS OF MIND

✹

For God has not given us the spirit of fear; but of power, and of love, and of a sound mind.
(2 Timothy 1:7)

Central Focus: God is not the author of confusion or a lack of mental clarity. He is the author of mental soundness, however.

Points to Ponder: God is renewing my mind. He is casting out all fear by His perfect love. I will let the mind of Christ take control of my mind. How I thank God that He has not given me a spirit of fear, but of love, power, and a sound mind. I will prosper and be in health, even as my soul prospers. As I focus my mind on God, His peace fills me up, because I trust in Him. (See Isaiah 26:3.)

Bible Meditation: By God's mercies to me I present my body as a living sacrifice, holy and acceptable to God, for I know that this is my reasonable service. I choose not to be conformed to this world, but to be transformed by the renewing of my mind that I may prove what is that good, acceptable, and perfect will of God.

I realize that the natural mind does not receive the

things of the Spirit of God, for they are spiritually discerned. I thank God that I have the mind of Christ which enables me to receive the things of the Spirit of God.

I choose to be like-minded with other believers, having the same love, of one accord, and of one mind. I will do nothing through strife or vainglory, but in lowliness of mind I will esteem others as better than myself. I will let the mind of Christ govern all my actions.

I am putting off concerning the former conversation the old man, which is corrupt according to deceitful lusts and I am being renewed in the spirit of my mind. I am putting on the new man, which after God is created in righteousness and true holiness.

Putting on the new man, which is renewed in knowledge after the image of Him who created us, involves putting on, as the elect of God, mercy, kindness, humility of mind, meekness, and longsuffering. I will forbear with others and forgive others. Above all else, I will walk in love which is the bond of perfection.

I will let the peace of Christ rule in my heart, to which I've been called and I will be thankful. I will let the Word of Christ dwell in me richly in all wisdom, and whatever I do in word or deed I will do all in the name of the Lord Jesus Christ, giving thanks to God and the Father by Him.

I will stir up the gift of God which is within me as I remember that He has not given me the spirit of fear, but of power, love, and a sound mind. Soundness of mind is my inheritance as a child of God. I am girding up the loins of my mind in full sobriety. I will hope to the end for the grace that is to be brought unto me at the revelation of Jesus Christ.

As I keep my mind stayed on the Lord, He extends His perfect peace to me. I will trust in Him forever, for He is everlasting strength for me.

There is now no condemnation for me, because I am in Christ Jesus and His mind is within me. I will walk after the Spirit, not after the flesh. The law of the Spirit of life in Christ Jesus has set me free from the law of sin and death, for what the law could not do, in that it was weak through the flesh, God sending His own Son in the likeness of sinful flesh and for sin, condemned sin in the flesh, that the righteousness of the law might be fulfilled in me, as I learn to walk after the Spirit. I am so thankful that the Lord has shown me that being carnally minded is death, but to be spiritually minded is life and peace. I choose to be spiritually minded because I know this gives me soundness of mind.

Scriptures: Romans 12:1-2; 1 Corinthians 2:14-16; Philippians 2:2-5; Ephesians 4:22-24; Colossians 3:10-17; 2 Timothy 1:6-7; 1 Peter 1:13; Isaiah 26:3-4; Romans 8: 1-6.

A Bible Prayer About Soundness of Mind: Heavenly Father, thank you so much for your love which casts all fear from me. I want the mind of Christ to guide me at all times. I know you will be my Guide even unto death. I pray, dear Father, that I would never allow my mind to be confused. Instead, I want to think on those things that please you. I will keep my mind stayed on you, and I know you will give me perfect peace as I do so. In Jesus' name I pray, Amen.

A Word of Wisdom: *"There is such a thing as having one's soul kept in perfect peace, now and here in this life; and childlike trust in God is the key to its attainment"* (Hannah Whitall Smith).

40

Spiritual Understanding

❧

*My mouth shall speak of wisdom; and
the meditation of my heart shall be of
understanding.*
(Psalm 49:3)

Central Focus: Wisdom and spiritual understanding
are closely related and they come to us as we
meditate upon the Scriptures.

Points to Ponder: God's Word opens our eyes
to spiritual understanding. This is far more than
knowledge; it involves following God's way and
seeing with His eyes. Spiritual understanding
comes from knowing Him, hearing His voice
speaking to us, and linking our hearts with His
wisdom. Fearing the Lord is the beginning of
wisdom, and this helps us to know that He is
always near to cheer, guide, and instruct us.

Bible Meditation: My mouth shall speak of
wisdom and the meditation of my heart shall
be of understanding. The fear of the Lord is the
beginning of wisdom. A good understanding have
all they that do His commandments. His praise
endures forever.

The Lord is giving me understanding, and this

is enabling me to keep His law. I shall observe it with my whole heart. He is making me to go in the path of His commandments. He is inclining my heart to His testimonies. He is establishing His Word to me.

The hands of the Lord have made me and fashioned me. He is giving me understanding that will help me to understand His commandments. God's words are sweet to my taste. They are sweeter than honey to me. Through His precepts I get understanding and this causes me to hate every false way.

I am so thankful that God is dealing with me as His servant. He is giving me understanding that I may know His testimonies. The entrance of God's Word into my spirit gives light and understanding to me. God's Word is very pure. Therefore, I love it.

The righteousness of God's testimonies is everlasting. He is giving me understanding that is enabling me to live. God is giving me understanding according to His Word. Great is my Lord, and He is of great power. His understanding is infinite, and He is sharing His understanding with me. Hallelujah!

With God's help I will know both wisdom and instruction, and I will perceive the words of understanding. I receive and believe God's Word and I hide His commandments within me. In so doing, I incline my ear to wisdom and my heart to understanding.

Wisdom enters my heart, and knowledge is pleasant to my soul. Discretion preserves me, and understanding keeps me. I will trust in the Lord with all my heart and not lean upon my own understanding. In all my ways I will acknowledge Him, and I know He will direct my steps.

I have found happiness because I have gained spiritual understanding. It is more precious to me than rubies and all the things I might desire cannot be compared with it. Length of days is in its right hand, and in its left hand are riches and honor. Its ways are ways of pleasantness, and all its paths are peace.

I will continue to seek wisdom and spiritual understanding. I will not forget them. Wisdom is the principal thing. Therefore, I shall get wisdom, and with all my getting I will obtain understanding.

Scriptures: Psalm 49:3; Psalm 111:10; Psalm 119:34–38; Psalm 119:73; Psalm 119:103–104; Psalm 119:125; Psalm 119:130; Psalm 119:140; Psalm 119:144; Psalm 119:169; Psalm 147:5; Proverbs 1:2; Proverbs 2:1–2; Proverbs 2:10–11; Proverbs 3:5–6; Proverbs 3:13–17;

Proverbs 4:5; Proverbs 4:7.

A Bible Prayer About Spiritual Understanding: Abba-Father, I thank you for all the wisdom and spiritual understanding you've imparted to me. It truly makes me happy and gives me a life that is far better than I ever thought possible. I will walk in your wisdom and spiritual understanding for the rest of my life. In your understanding I find peace and so many other blessings. Therefore, I will trust totally in you and not lean upon my own understanding any longer. Praise your mighty name. In the Savior's name I pray, Amen.

A Word of Wisdom: *"If we meditated more, we should live better. God help us so to do!"* (Charles Spurgeon).

41

STABILITY

❧

*But thanks be to God, which giveth us
the victory through our Lord Jesus Christ.
Therefore, my beloved brethren, be ye stedfast,
unmoveable, always abounding In the work
of the Lord, forasmuch as ye know that your
labour is not in vain in the Lord.*
(1 Corinthians 15:57-58)

Central Focus: God gives stability to us when we decide to put Him first and to follow Him at all times. He is the solid rock upon which we stand and He gives our life meaning and purpose.

Points to Ponder: Stability comes from standing on the Rock, which is Jesus Christ. We must learn to stand upon Him, His promises, and our commitment to Him. As we learn to stay rooted and grounded in Him, we will find stability for our lives. We will become steadfast and unmovable. We will always abound in His work. To do otherwise, would be double-mindedness, and every double-minded person is unstable in all his ways.

Bible Meditation: My heart is being knit together with the hearts of other believers in love and unto all riches of the full assurance of understanding, to the acknowledgment of the mystery of God, the Father, and of Christ, in whom are hid all the treasures of wisdom and knowledge.

In the same way that I have received Christ Jesus as my Lord, I will walk in Him (through faith). I am being rooted and built up in Him, and He is establishing me in the faith, as I have been taught, abounding therein with thanksgiving.

I am complete in Christ. All God's promises are Yes and Amen in Him unto the glory of God. He has established me with other believers in Christ, and He has anointed me and sealed me with the Holy Spirit.

In my heart I know I shall not be moved. I will bless the Lord who has given me His counsel. I have set Him before me; He is at my right hand, and I shall not be moved. Therefore, my heart is glad and my glory rejoices. My flesh shall also rest in hope. Hallelujah!

God is showing me the path of life, and in His presence there is fullness of joy. At His right hand there are pleasures forevermore.

Truly my soul waits upon God. My salvation comes from Him. He only is my rock and my salvation. He is my defense, and I shall not be moved. This is true stability for my life. He is my defense, and I shall not be moved.

In God is my salvation and my glory. He is the rock of my strength and my refuge. I will trust in Him at all times and pour out my heart before Him. He is my refuge forever.

God holds my soul in life and He does not permit my feet to be moved. He has proved me and tried me as silver is tried. I will lift up my eyes unto the hills from whence my help comes. My help comes from the Lord who made Heaven and Earth, and He will not permit my foot to be moved. He that keeps me will not slumber nor sleep. He is my keeper and the shade upon my right hand. The sun will not smite me by day, nor the moon by night. The Lord will preserve me from all evil. Indeed, He will preserve my soul. He will preserve my going out and my coming in from this time forth and forevermore. Hallelujah!

With God's help I will be steadfast, immoveable, always abounding in the work of the Lord, forasmuch as I know that my labor is never in vain in Him.

In faith, I ask God for wisdom, and I know He will give it to me. I do not want to waver in any, for I know that one who wavers is like the waves of the sea that are driven and tossed by the wind. A double-minded person is unstable in all his ways.

I want to be single-minded, so I will keep my mind stayed on God and trust totally in Him. In this way I will experience His perfect peace and spiritual stability in my life.

Scriptures: Colossians 2:2-3; Colossians 2:6-7; Colossians 2:10; 2 Corinthians 1:20-21; Psalm 10:6; Psalm 16:7-11; Psalm 62:1-2; Psalm 62:5-8; Psalm 66:8-10; Psalm 121; 1 Corinthians 15:58; James 1:5-8; Isaiah 26:3.

A Bible Prayer About Stability: Father-God, you are my stability. I take my stand upon you, my mighty Rock. I give my life to you afresh, and I ask you to fill me anew with the Holy Spirit that I might be faithful in everything concerning you and others. I praise you for all your promises that tell me that I will not be moved as long as I keep you before me. This I will do through your grace. In Jesus' name I pray, Amen.

A Word of Wisdom: *"Look to Him, look at Him, study Him, know all you can about Him, meditate upon Him"* (Charles Spurgeon).

42

STRENGTH

❦

God is our refuge and strength, a very present help in trouble. Therefore we will not fear, though the earth be removed, and though the mountains be carried into the midst of the sea.
(Psalm 46:1-2)

Central Focus: God's strength is always available to us, even in our moments of weakness. There is no strength greater than His.

Points to Ponder: I can do all things through Christ who strengthens me. He is my strength. In my weakness He is made strong. I need Him very desperately in my life. Without Him, I can do nothing. I will walk in the strength of the Lord at all times. He will see me through every situation, and He is always there to help me.

Bible Meditation: I love the Lord. He is my strength. He is my rock and my deliverer. He is my God, my strength, and the One in whom I trust. He is my buckler, the horn of my salvation, and my high tower. I will call upon Him. He is worthy to be praised.

He lights my candle and enlightens my darkness. By Him I have run through a troop and I have leaped over a wall. As for God, His way is perfect. The Word of the Lord is tried. He is a buckler to all those who trust in Him. He girds me with strength and makes my way perfect. He makes my feet like hinds' feet and sets me upon my high places. He teaches my hands to war, so that a bow of steel is broken by my arms.

Let the words of my mouth and the meditation of my heart be acceptable in your sight, O Lord, my strength and my redeemer. The Lord is my light and my salvation. Whom shall I fear? The Lord is the strength of my life. Of what shall I be afraid?

The Lord is my strength and my shield. My heart trusts in Him and I am helped. Therefore, my heart greatly rejoices and with my song I will praise Him. The Lord is the God of my strength. He is the strength of my heart and my portion forever.

The Lord reigns. He is clothed with majesty and with strength. I will seek the Lord and His strength. I will seek His face forevermore. The Lord is my strength and song. He has become my salvation. Blessed be the Lord, my strength, who teaches my hands to war and my fingers to fight.

The way of the Lord is strength to me. I will rejoice in Him and joy in the God of my salvation. He is my strength and He will make my feet like hinds' feet. He will make me to walk on the high places. God's grace is sufficient for me, for His strength is made perfect in my weakness.

I love the Lord. He preserves me. I will be of good courage, and He shall strengthen my heart. I humble myself under the mighty hand of God, and I know He will exalt me in due time. I cast all my cares upon Him, for I know He cares for me. I will be sober and vigilant, because my adversary, the devil, as a roaring lion, walks about, seeking whom he may devour.

I will resist him, steadfast in the faith. The God of all grace has called me unto His eternal glory by Christ Jesus. He is perfecting, strengthening, and settling me. To Him be glory and dominion forever and ever.

I will be strong in the Lord and in the power of His might. I will put on the whole armor of God, that I may be able to stand against the wiles of the devil. With God's help I will be strong in the grace that is in Christ Jesus.

Who is a strong Lord like my God? The fear of the Lord is a fountain of life, to depart from the snares of death. In the fear of the Lord I find strong confidence and a secure place of refuge. Hallelujah! The Lord God will come with His strong hand and His strong arm. He will feed His flock like a shepherd. He will gather His lambs with His arm and carry them in His bosom.

Knowing God, I will be strong and of good courage. I will observe to do according to all the Law. I will turn not to the right or the left, that I may prosper in everything I do and wherever I go. This book of the Law will not depart out of my mouth, but I will meditate in it day and night, that I will observe to do all that is written therein. Then my way will be prosperous and then I shall have good success.

Scriptures: Psalm 18:1-2; Psalm 18:28-34; Psalm 19:14; Psalm 27:1; Psalm 28:7; Psalm 43:2; Psalm 73:26; Psalm 93:1; Psalm 105:4; Psalm 105:4; Psalm 118:14; Psalm 144:1; Proverbs 10:29; Habakkuk 3:19; 2 Corinthians 12:9; Psalm 31:23-24; 1 Peter 5:6-11; 2 Timothy 2:1; Psalm 89:8; Proverbs 14:26-27; Isaiah 40:10; Joshua 1:6-8.

A Bible Prayer About Strength: O God, my strength, I come to you in my weakness, and I know you will fight the battle for me. I will be strong in you and in the power of your might. I will be of good courage through the power of your Spirit. I know it's not by might nor by my power, but by your Spirit that I shall prevail. Thank you for the victory I have in you. Now unto Him who is able to do exceeding abundantly above all that I could ever ask or think, according to the power that works within me, unto Him be glory in the Church throughout all ages, world without end. Amen. (See Ephesians 3:20-21.)

A Word of Wisdom: *"Through the study of books one seeks God; by meditation one finds Him"* (Padre Pio).

43

THANKSGIVING

❦

*Rejoice evermore. Pray without ceasing.
In every thing give thanks: for this is the will of
God in Christ Jesus concerning you.*
(1 Thessalonians 5:16-18)

Central Focus: Thankfulness abounds when we live close to God, because we experience His goodness in every part of our lives.

Points to Ponder: As we cultivate the attitude of gratitude, everything seems to change. We become more positive and we begin to focus on the blessings of God rather than the problems of life. A thankful heart is a merry heart, and a merry heart always does good like a medicine. (See Proverbs 17:22.) Rejoicing in the Lord is one of life's greatest experiences. The joy of the Lord is your strength. (See Nehemiah 8:10.)

Bible Meditation: I will serve the Lord with gladness and come before His presence with singing. He is my Creator. I am a sheep in His pasture. I will enter His gates with thanksgiving and go into His courts with praise. I will be thankful unto Him and bless His holy name, for He is good. His mercy is everlasting, and His truth endures to all generations.

I am thankful for God's peace that rules in my heart. I will ever be thankful for all He has done for me. I will let the Word of Christ dwell in me richly in all wisdom. I will teach and admonish others in psalms and hymns and spiritual songs, singing with grace in my heart to the Lord. Whatever I do in word or deed I will do all in the name of the Lord, giving thanks to God and the Father by Him.

I will praise the name of God with a song and I will magnify Him with thanksgiving. I will sing unto the Lord and make a joyful noise to the God of my salvation. I will come before His presence with thanksgiving and make a joyful noise to Him with psalms. My God is a great God, and He is a great king above all gods.

I will rejoice in Him always and be anxious about nothing. In everything with prayer and supplication with thanksgiving I will let my requests be made known unto Him. As I do so, His wonderful peace, which passes all understanding, will guard my heart and my mind through Christ Jesus. Hallelujah!

In the same way that I have received Christ Jesus as my Lord, I will walk in Him, rooted and built up in Him and established in the faith, as I have been taught, and I will abound therein with thanksgiving. I give thanks to God.

It is a good thing to give thanks unto the Lord and to sing praises unto His name. I will show forth His loving-kindness in the morning and His faithfulness every night. He has made me glad through His work. I will triumph in the work of His hands.

O death, where is your sting? O grave, where is your victory? The sting of death is sin, and the strength of sin is the Law. Thanks be to God, which gives me the victory through my Lord Jesus Christ. I will give thanks always for all things unto God and the Father in the name of my Lord Jesus Christ.

Blessing, glory, wisdom, thanksgiving, honor, power, and might be unto my God forever and ever. Amen.

Scriptures: Psalm 100; Colossians 3:15-17; Psalm 69:30; Psalm 95:1-3; Philippians 4:4-7; Psalm 75:1; Psalm 92:1-4; 1 Corinthians 15:55-57; Ephesians 5:20; Revelation 7:12.

A Bible Prayer About Thanksgiving: Father-God, I am so thankful to you for everything—past, present, and future. I thank you for always being there for me and with me. I thank you for setting me free from sin and Satan. I thank you for blessing me with all spiritual blessings in Christ Jesus. (See Ephesians 1:3.) I thank you for the grace that sustains me. Truly, your grace is sufficient for me. Thank you, Lord. In Jesus' name, Amen.

A Word of Wisdom: *"Faith sees God, and God sees faith. Faith sees God, who is invisible, and God sees even that little faith, which would be invisible to others"* (Charles Spurgeon).

44
TRUTH

❧

And ye shall know the truth,
and the truth shall make you free.
(John 8:32)

Central Focus: God cannot lie, for He is truth. We should always strive to be like Him, walking in truth and being truthful.

Points to Ponder: Jesus is the way, the truth, and the life, and no one is able to come to the Father unless they do so through Him. The Holy Spirit is the Spirit of truth. It is spiritual truth that sets us free, and it is true to say that truth is our best friend, no matter what the circumstances may be. God's Word is truth, and that's why we must spend time every day meditating upon it.

Bible Meditation: Jesus is the way, the truth, and the life, and no one can come unto the Father except through Him. Jesus promised me, "And you will know the truth, and the truth will make you free." I want to know the truth, as it is revealed in God's Word as fully as possible.

The Lord is showing His ways to me, and He is teaching me His paths. He is leading me in truth and teaching me. He is the God of my salvation and I wait on Him all day long. The Holy Spirit is the Spirit of truth, and He is my Comforter. He teaches me about Jesus. He will guide me into all truth, for He shall not speak of himself. Instead, He will speak what God reveals to Him. He will glorify Jesus.

God sanctifies me through His truth. God sends out His light and truth, and they lead me. They bring me unto His holy hill and into His tabernacles. The Lord desires for me to have truth in my inner parts, and it is there that I shall find wisdom. Hallelujah!

He is purging me with hyssop, and I am clean. He is washing me, and I am whiter than snow. He is causing me to know joy and gladness, and He is creating a clean heart and renewing a right spirit within me. He is restoring the joy of His salvation to me.

Mercy and truth are met together. Righteousness and peace have kissed each other. Truth shall spring out of the Earth, and righteousness shall look down from Heaven. God is teaching me His way through His Word. I will walk in His truth each step of the way. He is uniting my heart to fear His name. I will praise Him with all my heart, and I will glorify His name forevermore.

God is my refuge and my fortress. He is my God,

and I will trust fully in Him. He will deliver me from the snare of the fowler and from the noisome pestilence. He will cover me with His feathers, and under His wings shall I trust. His truth shall be my shield and buckler.

I will not be afraid of the terror by night, nor the arrow that flies in the daytime. I will not fear any pestilence or destruction. I have made the Lord my refuge and my habitation. He is giving His angels charge over me, to keep me in all my ways. They shall bear me up in their hands, lest I should dash my foot against a stone.

I will walk in His truth from this time forward.

Scriptures: John 14:6; John 8:32; Psalm 25:4–5; John 15:26; John 16:13–14; John 17:17; Psalm 43:3; Psalm 51:6–12; Psalm 85:10–11; Psalm 86:11–12; Psalm 91.

A Bible Prayer About Truth: Lord, your Word is the Word of truth and your Spirit is the Spirit of truth. I will walk in the truth they reveal to me, realizing that Jesus is the way, the truth, and the life for me. I love Him and I receive His truth as my shield and buckler. Thank you for your truth, which has made me free. Through your truth I have entered into the glorious liberty of the sons of God. (See Romans 8:21.) Thank you for the power of your truth, Father. In the name of Jesus, the

Savior, I pray, Amen.

A Word of Wisdom: *"I know not how God will dispose of me. I am always happy. All the world suffers; and I, who deserve the severest discipline, feel joys so continual and so great that I can scarce contain them"* (Brother Lawrence).

45
VICTORY

❧

*For whatsoever is born of God overcometh the
world: and this is the victory that overcometh
the world, even our faith.*
(1 John 5:4)

Central Focus: You are more than a conqueror
through Jesus Christ. He fights the battles for you,
and you will maintain His victory in your life when
you learn to trust Him each step of the way.

Points to Ponder: The victorious believer is one who
lives by faith, not by sight. He sees the important
things in life and knows how to use God's Word as
the sword of the Spirit, as he takes up the shield of
faith wherewith he is able to quench all the fiery
darts of the wicked one. Victory comes when we
learn to lean on God and let Him fight our battles
for us. He is the victorious One, and He lives within
us. Greater is He who lives within you than he who
is in the world. (See 1 John 4:4.)

Bible Meditation: I will sing a new song unto the
Lord, for He has done marvelous things. His right
hand and His holy arm have brought about the
victory. I will exalt God and praise His name, for He
has done wonderful things. His counsels of old are

faithfulness and truth. He has been a strength to the needy in his distress, a refuge from the storm, a shadow from the heat, and He will swallow up death in victory. The Lord God will wipe away all tears from all faces. Hallelujah!

The Lord has swallowed up death in victory. O death, where is your sting? O grave, where is the victory? The sting of death is sin, and the strength of sin is the Law, but thanks be to God, who gives us the victory through our Lord Jesus Christ.

Whoever is born of God overcomes the world, and this is the victory that overcomes the world, even my faith. Praise the Lord! I will overcome the world because I believe that Jesus is the Son of God.

The Lord will keep me. He will steady my feet. He enables me to prevail, for it is certain that by human strength shall no man prevail. I will seek first the Kingdom of God and His righteousness, and then all these other things will be added unto me.

I will remember that it is not by might, nor by power that I shall prevail. Through the Holy Spirit, however, I shall attain to victory in every situation. God girds me with strength and He makes my way perfect.

I will always love the Lord, my strength. He is my

rock and my fortress. He is my deliverer, my God, and my strength. I will ever trust in Him for victory and everything else I need. The Lord is my buckler, the horn of my salvation, and my high tower.

I will call upon the Lord who is worthy to be praised, so shall I be victorious over all enemies. The Lord sent from above and drew me out of many waters. He delivered me from my strong enemy and from all who hated me. The Lord is my stay. He brought me forth into a large place because He delights in me.

He will light my candle and enlighten my darkness. By Him I am able to run through a troop and leap over a wall. His way is perfect. His Word is tried. He is a buckler to all who trust in Him, and I trust in Him with all my heart.

God girds me with strength and victory. He makes my way perfect. He makes my feet like hinds' feet and He sets me on high places. He teaches my hands to war, and He has given me the shield of His salvation. His right hand holds me up and His gentleness has made me great.

He has enlarged my steps under me, so that my feet do not slip. He has girded me with strength for the battle and given me victory over all enemies.

Therefore, I will be strong in Him and in the power of His might. This will assure that victory shall be mine!

Scriptures: Psalm 98:1; Isaiah 25:1–8; 1 Corinthians 15:54–57; 1 John 5:4–5; 1 Samuel 2:9; Matthew 6:33; Zechariah 4:6; Psalm 18; Ephesians 6:10.

A Bible Prayer About Victory: Father, thank you so much for the victory you have given to me through my Savior, Jesus Christ. He has given me victory over sin, sickness, doubt, discouragement, and all negative influences. Faith is the victory that overcomes the world, and I will walk in faith from this time forth. I will walk in the victory you have provided for me. In Jesus' name, Amen.

A Word of Wisdom: *"Something greater than divine philosophy must link the heights and depths for man. It is faith. Faith lowers the heavens to earth"* (James Edward O'Mahony).

Pure Gold Classics
Timeless Truth in a Distinctive, Best-Selling Collection

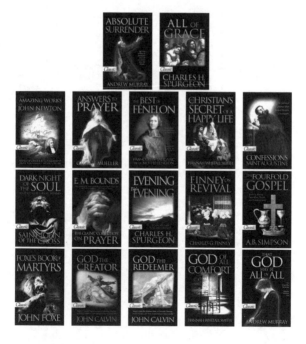

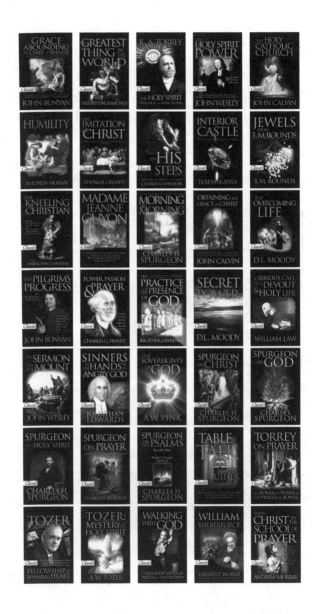

Prayers That Change Things

by Lloyd Hildebrand

More than 160,000 copies have been sold. These mass-market paperbacks contain prayers that are built from the promises of God and teaching that is thoroughly scriptural.

978-1-61036-105-7
MMP / 192 pages

978-0-88270-012-0
MMP / 232 pages

978-0-88270-743-3
MMP / 232 pages

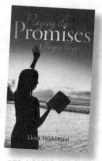

978-1-61036-126-2
MMP / 216 pages

978-1-61036-132-3
MMP / 248 pages